SPC

North Carolina

Also in the Spooky Series by S. E. Schlosser
and Paul G. Hoffman:

Spooky California

Spooky Campfire Tales

Spooky Canada

Spooky Maryland

Spooky Massachusetts

Spooky Michigan

Spooky Montana

Spooky New England

Spooky New Jersey

Spooky New York

Spooky Oregon

Spooky Pennsylvania

Spooky South

Spooky Southwest

Spooky Texas

Spooky Wisconsin

SPOOKY
North Carolina

Tales of Hauntings, Strange Happenings,
and Other Local Lore

RETOLD BY S. E. SCHLOSSER

ILLUSTRATED BY PAUL G. HOFFMAN

Guilford, Connecticut

Project editor: Jessica Haberman
Text design: Lisa Reneson, Two Sisters Design
Layout: Joanna Beyer
Map: M. A. Dubé © Morris Book Publishing, LLC

Library of Congress Cataloging-in-Publication Data

Schlosser, S. E.
  Spooky North Carolina : tales of hauntings, strange happenings, and other
local lore / retold by S.E. Schlosser ; illustrated by Paul G. Hoffman.
    p. cm.
  ISBN 978-0-7627-5124-2
  1. Haunted places—North Carolina. I. Hoffman, Paul G. II. Title.
  BF1472.U6S324 2009
  398.209756—dc22

                                                                2009013874

Printed in the United States of America
10 9 8 7 6

For my family: David, Dena, Tim, Arlene, Hannah, Emma, Nathan, Ben, Deb, Gabe, Clare, Jack, Chris, Karen, Davey, and Aunt Mil.

And for Mary Norris, Paul Hoffman, Erin Turner, Jess Haberman, and all the wonderful folks at Globe Pequot Press, with my thanks.

For Ralph and Cres Schultz, with my thanks for their hospitality. For Robbie, who tells a great story. And for Paul Roache and Gregory Brown, for their warm Boone welcome and wonderful tales.

Contents

MAP   x

INTRODUCTION   xiii

PART ONE: GHOST STORIES

1.   *Fetch*   2
BOONE

2.   *Daddy's Visit*   7
RALEIGH

3.   *The Nightmare*   14
OCRACOKE

4.   *Ghost Light*   21
MACO

5.   *The Little Red Man*   27
WINSTON-SALEM

6.   *Phantom Horseman*   33
GREENSBORO

7.   *I'm So Cold*   39
DARE COUNTY

8.   *The Handshake*   45
GOLDSBORO

9.   *Robah*   58
WINSTON SALEM

10.   *Busted!*   64
ASHEVILLE

11.   *The Rescue*   74
WILMINGTON

12.   *Plucked*   83
MURPHY

PART TWO: POWERS OF DARKNESS AND LIGHT

13. *Boo-Hag*   90
ELIZABETH CITY

14. *The Honeymoon*   97
THE SMOKY MOUNTAINS

15. *The Carpenter*   103
BAT CAVE

16. *Doppelgänger*   109
WATAUGA COUNTY

17. *Dreams and Visions*   115
PINEOLA

18. *The Coffin*   123
FAYETTEVILLE

19. *Resurrection*   128
CHARLOTTE

20. *The White Deer*   135
THE OUTER BANKS

21. *The Legend of Tsali*   141
SMOKY MOUNTAINS NATIONAL PARK

22. *Mercy*   148
SMITHFIELD

23. *Jubilee*   154
VANDEMERE

24. *Raven Mockers*   162
CHEROKEE

25. *The Cat*   173
EDENTON

RESOURCES   185
ABOUT THE AUTHOR   191
ABOUT THE ILLUSTRATOR   192

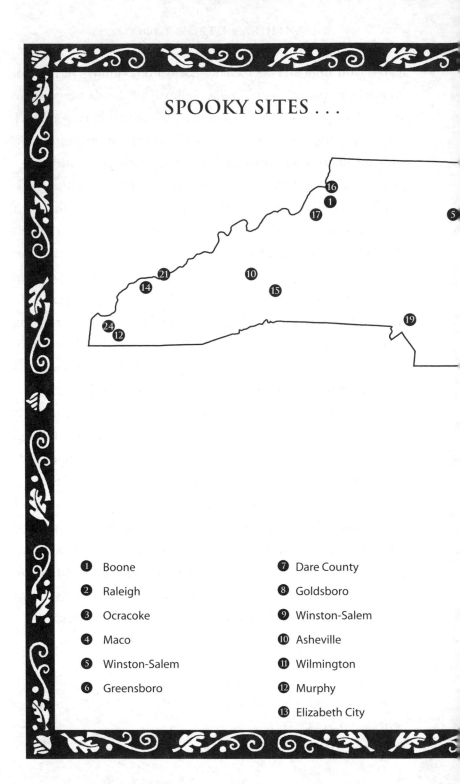

SPOOKY SITES . . .

❶	Boone	❼	Dare County
❷	Raleigh	❽	Goldsboro
❸	Ocracoke	❾	Winston-Salem
❹	Maco	❿	Asheville
❺	Winston-Salem	⓫	Wilmington
❻	Greensboro	⓬	Murphy
		⓭	Elizabeth City

AND WHERE TO FIND THEM

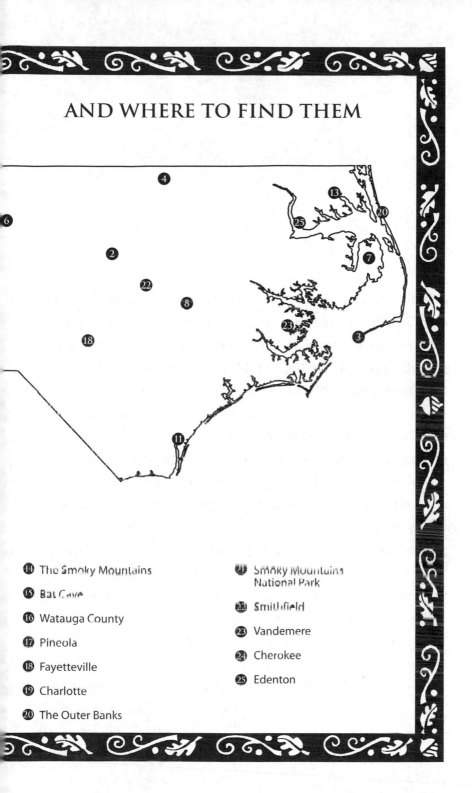

⑭ The Smoky Mountains

⑮ Bat Cave

⑯ Watauga County

⑰ Pineola

⑱ Fayetteville

⑲ Charlotte

⑳ The Outer Banks

㉑ Smoky Mountains National Park

㉒ Smithfield

㉓ Vandemere

㉔ Cherokee

㉕ Edenton

Introduction

The cool sea breeze tangled softly in my hair and brushed across my face as I stepped out of the car. I barely noticed, my eyes fixed in awe on the massive black and-white-striped Bodie Island Lighthouse looming over the clearing among its outbuildings, framed by the blue sky. The wind was whistling through the tall grass that lined the sand dunes behind the lighthouse and rustling in the trees as I pulled all my photography equipment out of the car and started snapping pictures in the warm January sunlight.

Bodie Lighthouse— which stands in Hatteras Island National Seashore in North Carolina—hadn't even been on my list of Things to Do when I set out from my gorgeous Outer Banks vacation "home away from home" that morning. My mind was all caught up in the excitement of visiting the Wright Brothers monument and seeing the First Flight exhibit at Kitty Hawk. I spent the whole morning re-creating the First Flight in my mind, walking the exact spot where the very first plane had taken off and landed under its own power, and watching in approval as a small-prop plane landed on the small airstrip next door. It seemed fitting to me that this place should still be used as an airstrip.

All at once, I felt tired and hungry. I had done enough research for one morning. Leaving the Wright Brothers behind,

I sat down to a nice leisurely lunch and then realized that the rest of the day was unplanned! This was a happy occurrence during my normally rushed spooky research trip. Getting back in my car, I pulled out onto the highway and proceeded to meander through the Outer Banks, stopping wherever my fancy took me. In this serendipitous way, I found a small beach overlooking the massive bridge between two of the Outer Banks islands. A single set of footprints wandered beside the blue waters of the Pamlico Sound, and a single seagull sat on a piling, resting easily in the sunlight. The footprints reminded me of the old folktale still told in this area of a young naval officer who encountered Blackbeard's headless ghost on an empty beach beside the Sound one dark night ("The Nightmare").

Then I found the lighthouse and had an impromptu photo shoot before taking a long walk on the beach. It was cold on the beach in January. I bundled up against the wind and started looking for empty skate cases and seashells along with a few other hearty souls who had ventured this way. I smiled as I strolled the emptiness of the beach, thinking that the current scene was a far cry from the crowds that lined the beaches of Vandermere during a Jubilee, when oxygen levels drop in the sea, causing crabs and flounder and fish of every description to rush for the

shore to find more air. The
harvest of all this bountiful
seafood involved everyone
in town, and it was not a
good place to lose a small
child, as one family had done
in a folktale I had collected
from the region. Unless of
course, the ghost of your
departed mother was there
to guide him back to safety
("Jubilee").

My wanderings in North
Carolina started long before
my happy day on the beach. I entered the state in the west,
staying my first night in Boone, where the spirit of a much-
loved dog once returned to bid his master farewell and play
one final game of "Fetch." From there, my search for spooky
folklore took me over Grandfather Mountain and down to
the town of Cherokee, situated on the eastern reservation of
that great nation. I spent a day there exploring the Smoky
Mountains National Park, though I was not privileged to meet
the spirit of Tsali, who still stands guard over his people in their
mountain homeland ("The Legend of Tsali"). While sad to miss
meeting the guardian spirit of the hills, I was very thankful not
to encounter "Raven Mockers," those terrible witches who stalk
the dying to steal their hearts and with them the remaining days
of their lives.

From the far west, I made my way to Asheville, once the
home to phony ghost busters who had the tables turned on

them when they visited a real haunted house ("Busted!"). I then headed to Charlotte to collect tales of long-ago Resurrectionists ("Resurrection"), who learned a hard lesson about the best way to earn spending money. Then it was onward to Winston-Salem to learn more about the ghost of "The Little Red Man," who once haunted the Single Brothers' house. And I found another great Winston-Salem story about the ghost of "Robah," who followed some adventurous college students home one Halloween night and started making mischief in the den.

North Carolina is so full of folktales that I could talk from dusk to dawn without touching on a third of them. There are stories of boo-hags, witches, devils, premonitions, phantom horsemen, doppelgängers, and more. Vengeance is a strong theme in several tales. An older brother kills his sibling and is visited each night by his brother's ghost, who plucks the hair right off his head ("Plucked"). A bride, abandoned at the altar, finally gets her man from beyond the grave ("The Handshake"). And a woman learns the hard way that she shouldn't steal the diamond engagement ring from her dead sister's hand ("I'm So Cold").

I received a warm welcome from everyone I met in North Carolina, and I heard many amazing and, of course, *spooky* stories. I've put my favorites in this collection. Enjoy!

—*S. E. Schlosser*

PART ONE
Ghost Stories

1

Fetch

BOONE

Clyde was the best dog I ever had. He was a black, gray, and tan German shepherd mix with a keen sense of smell and a quirky disposition. I loved him! He was always happy, always friendly. He went to every class I took at Appalachian State University, sitting at my feet and listening intently. After class, we would wander outdoors and play a game of fetch or go for a hike. Sometimes, we even studied. I would have aced every class if the professors had let *Clyde* take the tests.

Well, we graduated—Clyde with top honors, at least among the students—and had a brief hiatus in the Outer Banks. We loved the beaches and the wind and the waves, me and Clyde. But I was a mountain boy at heart, and the yen for the hills grew so strong within me that I came back to Boone. Clyde didn't mind where we were so long as we stuck together. I bought a nice little one-story ranch house with a full basement and, in time, brought home a bride to live there with the two of us. Sadly, my relationship with both Clyde and the little ranch house outlasted my relationship with my wife.

I was pretty devastated by the divorce, and it didn't help matters when my best buddy Clyde died of sheer old age. Tough, strong mountain man that I am, I bawled like a baby when I buried old Clyde in the front yard. There had never been another dog quite like him.

I stuck it out in the house for two years after the divorce but finally decided it was time to buy a condo and move on with my life. That little old house had too many memories, and no Clyde to soften them.

My sister and brother-in-law helped me pack up my things. On the day of the move, they loaded up their truck and headed off to the condo, leaving me to finish packing my own truck. I parked it on the street right in front of the house and trotted back and forth with packages and boxes, leaving the big old mirror that was propped opposite the front door for last, since it needed special packaging so that it wouldn't break during the trip.

I was down to the last few items when I stepped out of the door carrying a box and almost tripped over a stick laying smack-dab in the middle of the front walk. I frowned down at it. Where did that come from? It hadn't been there on my last trip out to the truck, and there was no wind that could have knocked it off a tree into the path. It was, I observed casually, just the type of stick that Clyde always favored when we played fetch—about a foot long and an inch thick. The wood had a knot at the center that looked like a cat's eye.

I felt a pang of loss when I saw the stick. Oh, how I missed Clyde. Adjusting the box on my hip, I scooped up the stick and threw it into the backyard, chucking it right over the low roof of the ranch house. Then I walked out to the truck and carefully loaded my box with the others.

Turning, I headed back toward the house to pick up the last few boxes. And there was the stick again, exactly where it had been before. My flesh crawled, and I felt goose bumps rising on my arms and legs. How had it gotten back here? It was the same funny old stick I'd just thrown over the house. I could tell by the knot at its center that looked like a cat's eye. I glanced around the yard, but no one was there. No way to explain the stick.

Hastily, feeling chills all over my skin, I picked it up and threw it over the roof of the house again. Then I headed in the front door. As I did, I glanced in the mirror propped up against the wall. In the bottom corner, standing reflected on the exterior walkway just where the stick had been, stood Clyde. His black and tan ears were pricked, his dark eyes glowed with delight, and his tail was wagging. There was no doubt it was Clyde.

Now I loved that dog more than anything. But seeing his ghost reflected in that mirror seriously freaked me out. I gasped, blinked, and then hurried to the bedroom to grab the final box off the bed. When I returned to the front hallway, there was nothing reflected in the mirror except empty walkway. I snatched up the old mirror any which way, locked the front door with shaking hands, and hurried down the walk to the truck parked out front. I didn't look down. I *really* didn't want to see if the stick was back.

A moment later, I was in the truck with the blasted old mirror tucked against the passenger's seat. My hands were shaking so badly that it took me two tries to get the engine started. Then the truck was in gear, and I was gone. Good-bye house. Good-bye old life. I hit my blinker and slowed for the left turn. Just

FETCH

before I rounded the corner, I glanced in the rearview mirror, staring back at the house. Was that a hint of black and tan by the walkway? The swish of a wagging tail?

A car rumbled past, cutting off my view. By the time I could see it again, the yard was empty.

Good-bye Clyde.

Daddy's Visit

It was a lovely spring afternoon, and I didn't hurry as I closed the front door behind me. I could smell lilacs in the air and stood for a moment on my small front porch breathing in the scent of spring. I heard birds chirping, a crow cawing in the tree, the whiz of a car passing in the street. And another sound, faint but distinct. The regular chuff-chuff sound of an engine warming up next door. I glanced over but saw no car in the driveway. That was odd. Was my new neighbor warming up the car in the garage? No, of course not. Any sensible person knew that was terribly dangerous. Carbon monoxide could build up fast. The car must be pulled up behind the house where I couldn't see it, I decided

A family of four had moved in next door about six weeks ago—a young couple in their thirties with two adorable little girls. I'd taken over an apple pie and introduced myself, and they seemed friendly enough. The father left for work before sunup each day and came home around three in the afternoon. He usually spent the time before dinner playing with his girls in the backyard while his wife rested or did errands, although for the last couple of days, it was the mother I saw outside in the afternoons.

I meandered down the front steps to my own car, parked out front in anticipation of my busy afternoon. I wanted to run a few errands before I started dinner. I took a last deep breath of lilac-scented air and then jumped into the car and headed off to the grocery store. I ambled my way through my errands, pausing to chat with a friend at the library, compare notes about fruit with a knowledgeable salesperson at the grocery, and discuss the best way to ripen tomatoes with the fellow manning the desk at the post office.

It was after 3:00 p.m. when I pulled into my driveway and parked the car by the back door. As I retrieved my groceries from the trunk, I heard the neighbor's car chuff-chuffing to itself next door. That was odd. Had they just returned from errands, as I had? Surely their car wasn't still warming up after two and a half hours?

Curious, I walked around the house and peered down my neighbor's driveway. I didn't see a car, but I could hear one running in the garage. Chuff-chuff-chuff. Rumble rumble.

I felt my skin prickling all over. It was very dangerous to run a car in an enclosed space. Even more so when the enclosed space was a garage attached to a house. Carbon monoxide could build up really fast. I stood there holding a couple of bags of groceries, wondering what to do. The soft rumbling sound made me uneasy. Abruptly, I dropped the groceries onto my front porch, walked back to their house, and rang the doorbell repeatedly. No answer. I knocked several times, first on the front door and then the back, calling the parents' names. Still no answer.

Now I was really worried. There was no sign of anyone home, and normally the kids would be out playing in the fenced-in

DADDY'S VISIT

backyard at this time of day. I phoned the house. No answer. I phoned both parents' cell phones. I got voice mail.

I couldn't leave things there. A car running in a closed garage was dangerous. Reluctantly, I called the police and explained the situation. They promised to send someone over, and I waited nervously for them on my front porch. It seemed to take forever for the police car with flashing lights to pull up. I ran at once to the car, babbling desperately about how I'd heard the car earlier but hadn't realized it was in the garage until I got home from my errands. "I think it's been running in there for over two hours," I concluded, almost wringing my hands in dread. The officer's face grew grim, but he spoke soothingly to me, asking me to wait for him on the porch. Then he went up to the house. I watched him ring the bell, knock, call. His partner did the same at the back door. Then they forced the garage door open. And found the young father dead in the car. He had committed suicide.

They called at once for an ambulance, and I heard them crashing into the house through the side door. From the sound of their shouts to each other, both little girls were inside the house and were suffering from the effects of carbon monoxide. The officers carried them out to safety, and I hovered in the background, watching helplessly as they did some preliminary first aid. The ambulance arrived within minutes—thank God— and the girls and their father were rushed to the hospital.

The mother arrived home just as the ambulance was pulling away. She ran toward the police officers in hysterics, demanding to know what had happened. She collapsed when she heard the news, and the officers asked me to go with her to the hospital after they had taken a brief statement from her.

On the way to the hospital, she told me she'd spent the day at a local spa. It was a birthday gift from her parents, and her husband had taken the day off to babysit the girls while she was away. Her husband suffered from clinical depression, but he had seemed so much better after they'd moved to the new house. "I never thought he'd do this," she whispered, scrubbing at her cheeks with a tissue.

When we arrived at the hospital, the doctors took the young mother aside and told her that her husband had been declared dead on arrival. As for the girls, the eldest daughter had been playing on the far side of the house from the garage and was the least affected by the carbon monoxide, but the little four-year-old was in a coma and was not expected to come out of it. Even if she did, the damage she appeared to have suffered was so extensive that she would never function normally again.

The young mother fell to pieces when she heard the news, and I felt terribly guilty myself. If only I had investigated the sound of the running car when I first heard it, I might have saved the life of that poor little girl at least. Now her father was dead, and she was dying. I tried to tell myself it was not my fault. But I didn't really believe it.

With my husband's blessing, I spent the night at the hospital with my neighbor and made arrangements for her parents—who lived overseas—to fly into Raleigh as soon as they could get away. When the older daughter was released in the morning, I brought her to our house to stay until her grandparents arrived from Europe. Her mother remained at the hospital night and day, sleeping in the pediatric intensive care room with her youngest child, praying for a miracle. We were all praying for a miracle, even as we helped with funeral arrangements for the poor young father who had suffered from a depression that neither his family's love nor medicine could lift.

Two days after the suicide, while my husband and our little houseguest drove to the airport to pick up her grandparents, I went to the hospital to see her mother and sister. While I was there, something strange happened. All night long, the poor tired mother had refused to leave her child alone in the room, not wanting her to wake up and find herself among strangers. So when I arrived, I volunteered to sit with the little girl while her mother washed up and had a rest. She thanked me with tears in her eyes and then went out into the hallway to ask the nursing staff where she could wash up and lie down for a few minutes.

I sat down in the chair by the bed, looking sadly at the sweet face of the tiny little girl sleeping her life away. This is not your fault, I told myself, though I did not believe it. I could hear the mother talking outside to the nurse as I sat there, watching the little girl breathe in and out, in and out. Suddenly, the temperature in the room dropped about twenty degrees. I shivered in the sudden cold, rubbing my arms to warm them. And then I was aware of an invisible presence entering the room. Footsteps came toward me, though I could see no one approach, and I felt someone walk past me. The invisible person actually bumped against my chair, shifting it forward a few inches. I heard the footsteps walk to the side of the bed and saw the dark hair on the little girl's head flatten as if a hand was patting it. The invisible hand swept a strand of hair off the child's cheek, and I heard a man's voice speaking words I couldn't understand. Then the presence was gone as suddenly as it had come. And in that instant the child's eyes popped open, and she sat up in bed.

I exclaimed in surprise, and my neighbor came running into the room with the nurse. And the little child who—it was supposed—would never speak again called out to her mother in a perfectly rational voice: "Mama! Mama!"

It was a miracle. There was no other word for it. The little girl held out her tiny arms, and her mother swept her up into a huge hug. The child hugged her back and said, "Daddy was here. He said he was sorry I had gotten hurt and that he missed me."

I swallowed hard when I heard her words. Was it her father I had just felt in the room with us?

The child continued: "Daddy told me I was going to be all right and that it was time for me to wake up. So I did."

I gasped. So did the nurse. My neighbor was crying—tears of joy for her daughter's recovery and of pain for the loss of her husband. As the nurse checked over her patient, I tiptoed quietly out of the room and left them alone. A great weight had rolled off my shoulders when the little girl awoke. The guilt I had felt at not reporting the running car sooner was gone now that she was awake and acting herself. Somehow, I knew everything was going to be all right. And it was all tied somehow to the visit from her father's ghost. He had not wanted his daughter to suffer because of his mistake, and he had come back to make things right.

I shivered a bit, spooked by the thought even as I was grateful for its result. Then I went to phone my husband with the good news

The Nightmare

OCRACOKE

The nightmare began almost as soon as I shut my eyes. I found myself crouching behind a water barrel on the deck of the *Ranger*, watching in heart-pounding fear as pirates swarmed aboard the ship. Seven, eight, nine, ten I counted. And the eleventh . . . My heart seemed to lodge itself in my throat, and I choked, clapping a hand over my mouth to keep the buccaneers from hearing me. He had a long beard that nearly covered his face. Tall and striking in appearance, the pirate wore a crimson coat with two bandoliers full of pistols and knives crossed on his chest, and two sharp swords at his waist. It was Blackbeard! A couple of cannon fuses stuck out from under his hat in my dream—something that hadn't happened in real life. They were hissing and spitting out smoke, creating such a terrifying aspect that I cowered, even in hiding.

Below decks, the hold was full of sailors waiting for this moment, but even that knowledge did not stop my heart from pounding in fear as the pirates spread out on the empty deck, their eyes searching for any sign of the crew. I screwed up my courage as best I could, waiting for the signal to attack. When it came, soldiers erupted from everywhere with shouts and loud battle cries.

THE NIGHTMARE

I leapt out from behind the barrel and charged into the fray, finding myself only a few feet from the mighty pirate captain. Blackbeard whirled to face me, his eyes alight with joy in the fight. He was huge, much taller than I and so fierce that my whole body trembled at the sight of him. I aimed my gun with shaking hands and stepped back a pace to regain my balance against a slight swell moving the ship. My foot landed on a rope instead of the flat boards of the deck. I stumbled, couldn't regain my balance, fell . . .

. . . And woke with my heart pounding so hard that it hurt my chest. In my head, the pirate's fierce black eyes still pierced through mine, and his pistol was raised to shoot me dead where I lay.

I was sweating like a pig under the blankets. My camp bed creaked as I turned over and fumbled for the lantern with shaking hands. It was three months later, and I still could not get that horrible moment out of my mind. We'd won the battle. We'd won. A shout from Lieutenant Maynard had distracted Blackbeard at the critical moment, turning him to face his arch enemy and giving me time to roll away to safety. I was back on my feet in time to see the two mighty men engage in battle. Yet in spite of my happy ending, the Blackbeard nightmare persisted. I knew he was dead. I'd ridden home on a ship with Blackbeard's severed head displayed prominently on the bow, and yet somehow . . .

Somehow, my mind refused to believe that the pirate was really dead. I kept reliving that fateful moment again and again. The skirmish had been over in a flash—just a few seconds of my life. But in my dream, every terrifying moment happened in slow motion. I saw again every minute expression on the pirate's face as he prepared to kill me. I felt my fingers gripping the gun, felt the slip of my foot on the rough rope, felt every motion as my body went down onto the deck. I thought I was dead. I would have been, had it not been for Maynard.

In the end, it was the nightmare that had brought me back to the Carolinas, to this small island of Ocracoke. I had heard reports from my fellow officers that the ghost of Blackbeard had been seen on the shores of the Pamlico Sound. He carried a lantern in his hand and searched the beaches for his lost head. It was just the sort of superstitious nonsense that always arose after a major battle. But this time I wanted to see for myself whether it was really true. I had nothing else to do. The nightmares were affecting my health so badly now that I'd been sent home on medical leave. Perhaps, I reasoned, if I saw the ghost of the pirate that haunted my dreams, my mind would finally be convinced that he was dead, and the nightmares would cease. Anyway, it was worth a try. So I sailed out to the island with a small tent, a camp bed, and provisions. And now here I was, awakened again by the nightmare, just in time to go out along the shores of the sound and watch for a ghost that probably did not exist.

With a sigh I rolled out of bed, dressed myself warmly against the sea winds, and went to sit on the dunes near my tiny fire. A million stars wheeled over my head as I gazed quietly upward. A wisp of a moon was already low on the horizon, getting ready to set. I listened to the swish of the wind in the long grasses, the lapping of the waves in the sound. Somewhere close, crickets chirped and night creatures hunted. It was peaceful and soothing, a far cry from my nightmare. I really wasn't expecting to see anything as I pulled a blanket around my shoulders and deeply breathed the fresh air.

I don't know how long I was sitting there in a half-doze when I realized that one of the stars low on the horizon was moving toward me. I blinked in confusion and watched it for a while. Then I realized I was seeing a lantern. Someone holding a lantern was strolling up from the beach. Pulse pounding, I wondered, *Is it Blackbeard?* Then common sense reasserted itself. It couldn't be. Okay, maybe I'd come here to see a ghost. But in reality, I didn't believe that ghosts existed. And even if I did, they certainly never appeared on command (they are a lot like children in that respect). I certainly wasn't expecting a ghost sighting on the first night of my stay.

In spite of these reassuring thoughts, my body was sweating with fear as the footsteps approached. Then I made out the face of one of the local fishermen, lit by the lantern, and I had to chuckle at myself. Relieved (and a little disappointed), I called a greeting. He came up to me, and we shook hands. He was out night fishing and had come to my campsite to issue me an invitation to join his family for Sunday dinner—which was scheduled for noon the next day. I accepted the invitation gratefully. A hot, home-cooked meal was always welcome to a traveler. We sat for a couple of minutes talking about this and that before he made his way back to his fishing boat. I walked down to the boat with him and bade him good fishing. Then I watched him row out into the sound, his lantern a bobbing light that faded slowly into the night.

I stood for a while, letting my eyes adjust to the darkness. Then I turned and walked slowly back toward my camp, smiling a little at the supernatural fear I'd felt at the sight of that lantern. Suddenly, I accidentally bumped into someone passing me in the dark. "I beg your pardon," I said automatically as I stepped aside for the person to pass.

"Watch where yer walking," a voice grumbled back from the darkness, and I felt the swish of a large body pressing close to mine. I froze suddenly in mind-numbing fear. I was standing on a wide-open, empty beach under the glimmering starlight. How could I have bumped into someone? I was the only one there. And yet I heard the crunch of footsteps on the sand behind me, as that someone kept walking. Swallowing hard, I turned around—and saw nothing but empty beach and the wide darkness of the water, glimmering softly in the starlight.

Then a blue light glowed suddenly, as if the cover on a dark lantern had been lifted. It blinded my eyes with its dazzle. I lifted a hand to shield my gaze and caught a glimpse of a crimson coat with two bandoliers full of pistols and knives crossed on a broad chest, and two sharp swords at a thin waist. But I saw no bushy black beard. The phantom had no head at all. Just a bloody stump where its head should be.

"My head . . . Where's my head?" The glowing blue figure howled the words aloud, its voice a heart-wrenching shriek in the darkness. How it could speak without a mouth I would never know. Nor did I care to find out.

My feet were much smarter than my brain. They had me heading up the dunes toward my fire and my tent while my head was still turned back toward the beach, staring at the ghost. The phantom vanished suddenly with a popping sound. I gave a shriek that would have shamed a banshee and dove headfirst through the door of my tent. I huddled for a long time under my camp bed before, shamefaced, I crept into it and went to sleep. After all, I reasoned as my shaking slowly ceased, I had come here to see a ghost. I shouldn't act like such a coward when it actually happened.

That night, for the first time since the battle, I slept without dreams. And when I awoke, I knew I was cured. At least of the first nightmare! I wasn't sure how I was going to cure myself of the vision of the ghost. I shook like a frightened child whenever I recalled it.

Completely overcome by my Blackbeard sighting, I packed up my belongings as soon as I awoke and loaded them into my small sailing skiff. Then I spent the morning fishing as far away from the haunted beach as I could go and still keep my promise to have dinner with the fisherman and his family at noon. It was a wonderful meal, and I heartily wished I had been able to enjoy it. But every mouthful tasted like sawdust to me, so deep was my longing to get away from the island.

As soon as common courtesy would allow, I bade farewell to my host and hostess and sailed away from the haunted dunes overlooking the Pamlico Sound, never to return there during the length of my days. I did not want to risk having a third encounter with the legendary pirate. Two meetings were more than enough!

4

Ghost Light

MACO

I thought the kids would get a big kick out of it when I suggested we stop on the way to the seashore to watch for the Maco Light. After all, kids like spooky stuff. But they were dubious about the proposition, and my wife, Amanda, was downright skeptical.

"Why do you want to watch for some old ghost light?" she complained. "I thought you didn't believe in that stuff."

"I'm a skeptic. Seeing is believing," I replied.

The kids chimed in then. My daughter, Lily, was eager to see the ghost light, but Kevin Junior just wanted to get to the beach.

"We won't get there till after dark anyway. You won't be able to go to the beach until tomorrow," I said firmly. And that was that. Kev rolled his eyes expressively at my authoritarian manner and then subsided into a sulk in the backseat. Teenagers! When I complained to my own father about my teenager, he laughed at me and told me my mother had wished him on me. Apparently, I was just the same when I was a kid.

It was dusk by the time we neared our destination. I switched on the car headlights and turned down the road toward Maco. To get the kids in the mood, I told them the story of the Maco Light in my best spooky manner.

There was once a railroad conductor named Joe Baldwin who was working for the newly rebuilt Atlantic Coast Line. The year was 1867, and the railroad had expanded to include a small station in Maco, North Carolina. Joe was assigned to the very last car in the train, and he executed his conductor duties to the best of his abilities aboard his assigned car. Then one night, something went wrong. Terribly wrong. The train was heading down the line toward the tiny Maco station when Joe's car started to slow down dramatically. Worried, Joe went forward to see what was happening, and he realized that his car had become decoupled from the rest of the train. Joe's heart leapt into his throat when he saw the retreating lights of the train disappearing into the distance. His car was stuck on the tracks, and another train was following close behind them.

With a shout of dismay, Joe grabbed his signal lantern and frantically ran the length of the car. Bursting out of the back door, he ran out onto the rear platform. Yes, he could see the next train speeding toward them down the track. By the look of it, the engineer had not realized the danger. Joe leaned over the rail, desperately signaling for the engineer in the following train to stop. But the train barreled forward, its speed unabated. Joe realized that the engineer must not have seen his signal light— or perhaps had not realized its significance. He kept waving the lantern frantically from side to side, shouting in vain over the huge rumbling force of the oncoming train. The engine grew larger and larger, and Joe's heart was in his throat as he realized the train was not going to stop.

With a thunderous roar and the great shriek of massive metal hitting massive metal, the engine struck the helpless car. Joe, still at his post, was smashed between the two trains; his head was severed from his body. The signal lantern flew wildly out of his hand, rolling along beside the tangled metal of the two trains and miraculously flipping upright, still alight. Joe was the only fatality in the railway accident that night. The railroad officials never located his head.

Shortly after the train accident, the Maco Light began to appear on the tracks near the station. People traveling on the train, or crossing the tracks at Maco, would report a light shining in the distance when no train was due. The light would appear as a small ball, far down the tracks, and then would come closer and closer to the observer until it was the size of a lantern. People reported that the light moved back and forth frantically, as if it were signaling a train to stop, just as Joe Baldwin had done the night of the accident.

The phenomenon became so common that the Atlantic Coast Line Railroad ordered their engineers not to stop for the light if they saw it as they were approaching Maco. Folks believed it was the spirit of Joe the conductor, desperately replaying his final moments over and over again, trying to get the following train to stop before it hit his helpless car.

As I finished the story, Kevin Junior gave an annoying and rather dramatic sigh and said, "Boring." I ignored him and turned into the pull-off beside the railroad tracks. It was a dark night, and it got even darker as I shut down the engine and turned off the lights.

"My teacher said President Grover Cleveland saw the Maco Light once in 1889 when he was riding the train," Lily piped up from the backseat.

"That's right," I said enthusiastically, tossing her a happy smile over my shoulder.

GHOST LIGHT

We were the only ones at the pull-off that night. The moon had already set, and it was very dark. There were no vehicles passing on the lonesome highway, and all I could hear were the swish of the wind and the rattle, buzz, chirp, and bump of night creatures in the woods. I leaned back in my seat and waited, watching the faint glimmer of the railroad tracks in the starlight.

"This is boring," said Kevin after ten minutes of silence.

"Then take a nap," I suggested.

Ten more minutes passed. An owl hooted back in the woods, and Lily jumped. "What was that?" she whispered. Kevin laughed at her. "It's just a boring owl," he said.

Ten more minutes went by. "Honey, that dratted light is not going to show itself tonight," Amanda said "Let's go."

And then a small dot of white light appeared far down the railroad tracks. My chest tightened in excitement, and my heart started to pound against my ribs. "Look at that! Look!" I said hoarsely, pointing. Everyone looked, even Kevin.

"It's just someone with a flashlight," Kevin said a bit uncertainly after a moment. We ignored him, breathlessly watching as the light moved slowly forward, getting larger and brighter as it approached.

At first I was excited to see it. Then goose bumps raised on my skin, and I began to feel a bit . . . well, creepy. There was something disconcerting about a light with no source coming closer . . . closer. Nothing was behind it or above it or below it to explain why it was there. Nothing at all. At least nothing I could see.

I could feel my whole body trembling. Beside me, Amanda gripped my arm so hard it hurt. "Make it stop, Daddy. Make it stop," Lily whimpered from the backseat. The light hovered at man-height above the ground and was now the size of a lantern. Then it started frantically moving from side to side, as if it were signaling. And no one was holding it! No one at all.

My heart was hammering so heavily that it actually hurt my chest, and my throat felt so tight that I could not make a sound. Even my legs started to shake. For a moment it looked as if the light would come right into the car with us! I was reaching trembling hands for the keys when the light vanished abruptly, just a few feet from our car.

Everyone gasped in fear and relief. Amanda loosened her grip on my arm. "Where did it go?" Lily asked at the same moment that Kevin said, "Maco Ghost Light! That was cool! Can we do it again?"

I cleared my throat a couple of times. "I think once is enough for tonight," I managed to say in a voice that sounded a few pitches too high.

"Once is enough for forever," Amanda muttered.

"Let's head to the hotel," I said in a more normal tone as I started the car and turned back onto the highway. I needed to see people milling about, streetlights that had a source, and the other trappings of normal society. The sight of that bodiless light floating toward me would haunt my dreams for quite a while, and I was not sure I wanted to see it again.

Like Amanda said, some things you do only once.

5

The Little Red Man

WINSTON-SALEM

It was amazing how these folktales sprang up, the visitor mused, accepting a cup of coffee from the serving girl. He sat back in his chair, eyeing his friend askance. Frankly, it surprised him to hear a prominent member of the Moravian Church talking about a ghost. He had not thought that the church would approve of the telling of such tales.

The town of Salem had been settled by the Moravian church in 1766, as part of the North Carolina Wachovia settlement. The Moravians were a Protestant sect with a strong missionary focus, and the church played a central role in their lives. The church strictly divided the members of its congregation by sex. Men and women sat in separate sections of the church during services and the unmarried men and women in the church were divided into "Choirs" (groups classified according to age and sex). Several houses were created to care for the spiritual and temporal welfare of the Choirs. These included the Houses of Single Brethren, Single Sisters, and Widows. It was only after a marriage took place that families were allowed to live together under one roof.

According to his friend—one of the more prominent citizens in Salem—it was one of these Houses that had become famed for its ghost. Its ghost! How ridiculous.

"It really is a most interesting tale," the Salem citizen mused, taking a sip of coffee from his cup.

The visitor raised a skeptical eyebrow at him.

The Salem citizen laughed: "I know you don't believe in ghosts, *mein Freund,* but listen to the tale yourself, and then decide!" He went on to relate the ghostly tale in full.

Brother Andreas Kramer was a single man working as a shoemaker and living in the Single Brothers' dormitory in town. He was a happy little man who walked the streets of Salem with his red cap perched jauntily on his head. He would nod cheerfully to everyone he met, and the children in town all loved him for his playful spirit and good heart.

One evening in March, Brother Kramer—who had been uncommonly quiet all day—joined a few of his brothers in the excavation of the new cellar for the extension to the Single Brothers' house after attending the evening services. The men were cutting into the earthen bank and then pulling down the overhang. It was an excavation technique that had been successfully used in the past, but some brothers doubted the wisdom of using it for this particular cellar, because of the sandy nature of the soil.

However, the brothers who objected to this method were overruled by the majority, and thus it was that Brother Kramer and several other men were kneeling under the overhanging bank when it collapsed. The other men made it out safely, but Andreas was buried. Frantically, the men dug into the cave-in, trying to rescue their friend. A hint of red cloth became visible in the lantern light, guiding their digging. A few moments later, the owner of the red cap was visible underneath the dirt and debris that had buried him. But when the poor shoemaker was gently pulled out of the rubble, it was obvious that he was dying. One leg was twisted and broken, and he seemed to be suffering from internal injuries as well. The cave-in happened at midnight, and by 2:00 a.m. the shoemaker was dead.

Every member of the Moravian Church was saddened by the loss of the cheerful little man in the red cap. What they didn't expect was the sudden flurry of supernatural activity in the Single Brothers' house after the death of Andreas the shoemaker. The men digging out the cellar and building the new addition often sensed the presence of someone working beside them, even when they were quite alone. The tap-tap-tap sound of the shoemaker working in his dorm room still rang through the building occasionally, making the Single Brothers smile. And every once in a while, the men would hear the patter of footsteps, just before a partially transparent little man in a red cap slipped past an open doorway and vanished down the hallway.

Pausing to take another sip of coffee, the Salem man grinned at his visitor. "Would you like to hear more?" he asked. Gruffly, pretending disinterest, the visitor nodded and beckoned to the serving girl to refill his coffee cup.

After a time, the Salem citizen continued, the haunted house was no longer needed for the Single Brothers, so it became a home for several families to share and eventually became a home for widows. The widows liked to giggle and gossip about the little red-capped fellow they sometimes saw in the hallway. One time, when a little deaf girl came for a visit to her granny, the child asked the old woman about the "funny little red man" whom she had seen several times in and around the house. The old woman

THE LITTLE RED MAN

was astonished. Her granddaughter had lost her hearing as a tiny child and knew nothing of the story of Brother Kramer, yet here she was asking about the ghost as if she had really seen him!

The Salem citizen paused again and grinned at the visitor. "Pretty strong evidence, that!"

The visitor snorted. "If you like," he grunted in disbelief.

"Well, then, let us pay a visit to the house," the Salem man said with a smile. "You are a builder by trade, and the house has some very interesting subcellars you might be interested in viewing, including the one that was instrumental in that fatal accident so long ago. And who knows, we may even catch a glimpse of a red cap!"

The visitor chuckled in polite disbelief but acceded to the plan. Permission from the widows was quickly granted, and the two men went down to the sub-basement level. The visitor was soon absorbed in the architecture of the place, asking interested questions about the excavation and construction of the building.

When they reached the fatal cellar, the Salem man pointed to the place where the collapse had happened and reiterated the story of the little Red Man. The visitor gave a polite snort, turned, and then froze in place with a gasp. The temperature in the air around the men dropped more than twenty degrees in a second, and before their eyes was a small, wiry man wearing a red cap. His feet were a good six inches above the floor of the cellar, and he folded his arms and mimicked the visitor's disbelieving frown to perfection.

The visitor felt his flesh creep in reaction to this strange visitation, but he was a brave man and forced himself to move forward toward the apparition. "Let's see if you're really real," he said in a voice that was just a shade higher than his normal pitch. The visitor lunged at him and stepped right through his body. It felt like being stabbed by a thousand icicles all at once. The visitor gasped and bent over for a second against the horrible sensation that was almost painful in its intensity. When he recovered a bit, he glanced back over his shoulder.

"I told you," the Salem man said from behind him. The Salem man hadn't moved a muscle when the ghost appeared. He was sweating a little but wore a half-smile too. The visitor frowned at him. "Somebody's playing a trick on us," he said. "I just can't figure out how they made the feet appear as if they didn't touch the ground."

"If you like," the Salem man said in polite skepticism.

There came a tap-tap-tap from the doorway. The visitor whirled around. The little Red Man hovered in the doorway, grinning from ear to ear, and happily saluted the visitor from the doorway. His feet still did not touch the ground. Then he vanished with a small popping noise.

The visitor's eyes met those of the Salem man. They stared at each other for a long moment—the one ashen, the other smiling.

"All right," the visitor said at last. "I will grant you a ghost. Now let's get out of here!"

The Salem man laughed. Then he took the visitor away to the tavern and offered him a drink to sooth his jangled nerves.

Their encounter with the ghost became a favorite story of the Salem citizens in later years, even after a visiting minister laid the ghost to rest. The Salem man wasn't sure if he should be happy or sorry that the ghost was gone. Still, it made a fair tale, even from the far side of the vale.

Phantom Horseman

Some things you just don't anticipate. I didn't anticipate finding myself homeless after the divorce. But somehow, my ex-wife ended up with the house and the car, and I ended up homeless with a golden retriever to feed.

After a bit of fancy footwork, I got a small place in Greensboro near a local park, which had some good walking paths. Jeeter and I jogged together every day, and our new neighborhood, with its easy access to the park, was a wonderful place to do it. Shortly after moving in, I learned that the park and all of the area surrounding it—including my house—had been the site of a Revolutionary War battlefield. Unfamiliar with the story, I did some digging at the local library to learn more and was intrigued to discover that my property had some historical significance.

The Battle of Guilford Courthouse took place between the British troops, led by Major General Lord Cornwallis, and the Continental Army, led by Major General Nathanael Greene. According to the history books, Cornwallis was chasing the Continental Army through the Carolinas, trying to defeat them. Greene stayed well ahead but chose this particular vicinity to make his stand. He set up three battle lines, and

Cornwallis rushed to attack him on the morning of March 15, 1781, by which time his troops were hungry and tired. The British advanced up a road through thickly wooded country to an area cleared for grazing, where they engaged the first of three lines of American soldiers. The British broke through all three lines after heavy fighting on both sides and sent the Continental Army into retreat, although the casualties inflicted on the British made it more of a defeat for them than a decisive victory.

I told the story to Jeeter during our jog the morning after I'd done my research. Jeeter was not impressed. I guess he would prefer to live on a battlefield where the American troops had defeated the British. Still, as I told him, Greene's men had harassed Cornwallis's army so badly that they never recovered, and shortly thereafter they were defeated at Yorktown—ending the Revolutionary War in our favor.

We'd been in our new home for three months when Jeeter brought me the leash one evening, wagging his golden tail enthusiastically. We'd jogged already that morning, but he wanted to go out again. Since I had no big plans for the evening, a walk seemed like a pleasant idea. We wandered down the street as we listened to the soft chirping of crickets and the call of night birds from the dark trees in the park, which backed all the houses on the street. It was a lovely warm evening, strangely bereft of human company. The houses on either side of us were silent and dark, and the soft whistle of the wind was the only noise aside from the rustle of night creatures in the park.

Abruptly, Jeeter stopped walking. The hair bristled up all along his back, and he growled. I glanced ahead, following his gaze. A shadowy figure had appeared on the darkened street between the pools of light that came from the lampposts. I heard a clip-clop, clip-clop noise coming toward me. It sounded like hoofbeats—a strange thing to hear in this modern place. Was someone riding a horse toward us?

Jeeter's tail clamped suddenly between his back legs. He gave a whimper of fright and cowered behind me, tangling me up in his leash so tightly that I couldn't move. I just stood there, watching a dark figure approaching me on horseback while my dog trembled against my legs. The horseman rode under a streetlight, and I saw him clearly for the first time. He must have been doing a historical gig for one of the local schools, because he was dressed in the uniform of a Continental soldier. He had his part down perfectly, looking about as tattered and weary and heartsore as any man might who was part of a defeated army.

"Good eve, young sir," the man called to me.

"Good evening," I replied cautiously. The breeze arose around us. Now it felt cold on my skin, and I shivered, my arms suddenly prickly with goose bumps. I was filled with the strong desire to flee to the safety of my own house. I dismissed this ridiculous notion as the horseman reined in his beast beside me. He sat looking at me in silence for a moment. It was uncanny. I felt as if I were caught up in a strange tableau, or a painting of some kind. I was frozen in place and could do nothing to remove myself from this encounter.

Jeeter whined against the back of my tangled legs. I felt my heart pounding and my flesh crawling under the soldier's stare.

"This place, these houses," the soldier said finally, gesturing with the whip in his hand. He seemed to be pointing directly

PHANTOM HORSEMAN

at my house, even though it was several yards down from our present location. "They have been built on the bodies of the slain."

I glanced around me. I had never thought of that. I supposed it must be true. Many people had died in this place during the battle.

I nodded. "I believe you are right," I said cautiously, absently stroking my dog's head, as much to comfort myself as to comfort him.

The horseman looked me straight in the eye. Under the streetlight, he appeared pale, almost ethereal, as if he were not quite real. "It is not good to desecrate this place. Do not disturb the dead," he said sternly. And he vanished.

Jeeter trembled violently against my legs. I gave a yelp of surprise and felt the spell that had paralyzed me evaporate suddenly. I turned abruptly, forgetting the tangled leash, and fell over Jeeter. For a moment all was tangled leash, sweaty dog, and swearing owner. Then we were both on our feet and running for home in great leaps and bounds. Jeeter beat me to the front door by a hair's breadth and whined at me while my shaking hands fumbled with lock and key. We stumbled inside, and I slammed the door behind us and leaned against it.

"A ghost," I gasped aloud. "That man was a ghost." I glanced around for Jeeter, but my dog had vanished. I found him later, cowering under the bed.

I kept waking up that night, cold shudders running across my skin, hearing the phantom's final words over and over in my mind: "Do not disturb the dead."

I rose in the morning heavy-eyed and unready for the morning jog. Jeeter, who normally woke me with leash in mouth and tail wagging, was visibly absent. He was still under the bed and refused to come out.

I left for work without going for a jog and jumped every time someone spoke to me at the office. When I got home, Jeeter was still under the bed. That decided me. I went to the closet, pulled out a suitcase, and began packing. "We're getting out of here," I told my dog.

Jeeter must have understood. As soon as I was packed, he crept out from under the bed with his leash in his mouth and trotted to the back door. I hauled the suitcase after him, and a minute later we drove away from that haunted neighborhood and didn't look back. I hired movers to pack up my place—I had nightmares just thinking about setting foot in that house again—and settled over in Winston-Salem with my dog.

We never returned to that haunted street.

7

I'm So Cold

DARE COUNTY

Mary and Kate were two sisters who were mighty close for kinfolk. They married two brothers and lived on the same street in the same little town, and their kids always played together. It was something to see. Not many folks get along so well with their kin!

But Mary had a secret that no one knew about—not even Kate. 'Specially not Kate. Ya see, Mary was jealous o' Kate's man. Not that she wanted him fer herself. Nope, what she wanted was the money he brought home to Kate. The brother Mary married weren't no good with finances, and Mary's clothes and shoes and house weren't half as nice as Kate's.

All this jealousy, in the end, focused on one item. Mary became kinda obsessed with the fancy diamond ring her brother-in-law put on his wife's hand the day they married. 'Course, Mary hid her feelin's real well. Sometimes, she'd stare at her sister's hand when Kate was busy with her little son—who was an only child. And once she asked to try on the diamond ring, which fit Mary perfectly. But other than that, she didn't say nothing. After all, Kate and her husband were mighty generous, and they bought Mary and her young 'uns gifts all the time.

I'M SO COLD

Still, that jealousy festered and festered in Mary through the years as the young 'uns grew up and left home. Then Mary's husband died, followed shortly by Kate's man, and the two sisters moved in together fer company. And that's when things got bad. Mary started making nasty remarks about Kate havin' money. Kate was terrible surprised. Here she was, thinkin' Mary loved her unconditional-like, and her sister had done fooled her all these years. Kate was real hurt. She moved out of the house the very next morning and didn't come back.

So Mary lived all alone in her little house, growin' meaner and more cross every day. Mary didn't see no one for days on end but the grocer boy and the milkman. Her young 'uns lived far away and never really writ or visited. When her daughters did phone, Mary done her best to poison their minds against their terrible Aunt Kate, sayin' that she'd left Mary to fend all alone and went to live the posh life with her son in Raleigh.

Then the nephew called to tell Mary that Kate had passed. He sounded real sorry to lose his Ma, and he dint know nothing about a quarrel between the sisters. Mary felt a pang about that in the region where her heart was supposed t'be. Here she were, thinkin' Kate had poisoned her nephew against his aunty, and it weren't so. Mary'd done her best to poison her daughters against Kate, and both of them refused to come to the funeral on account of it. But Mary went all the way to Raleigh, where her nephew had lived with his Mama until she passed. She helped lay out the body and picked out Kate's nicest outfit to dress her in. And Mary took the diamond ring off Kate's finger when her nephew weren't lookin', figuring Kate didn't need it no more.

They buried Kate the next mornin', and Mary went back to her little house to gloat over her diamond ring. And not jest the diamond ring. According to her nephew, Kate had laid by a tidy sum jest fer her sister. Mary felt a little bad about that, but not enough to stop her enjoying the new ring. She loved to watch it sparkle on her hand.

That night, Mary woke suddenly in her dark bedroom, sure she'd heard someone call her name. She blinked up at the ceiling, realizing that there was a glow comin' from her doorway. She rolled over, wonderin' if one of her daughters done come in the night without phonin' her first. But it weren't her daughter. Floating in the hallway, outlined by the frame of the open doorway were a glowing blue figure. "Mary," it called. "Mary! I'm c-c-cold, Mary!"

Mary's heart started banging against her chest, and she broke out into a cold sweat. She knew that voice. She hadn't heard it since the day of the argument, dontcha know, but she recognized it. The blue figure was the ghost of Kate.

Mary rolled over quickly and pulled the covers over her head, pretending she dint hear nothing. "G'way ghost," she muttered. "G'way. I don't have nothing of yers." She felt a swirling breeze brush her fingertips where they clutched the eiderdown over her head. She pulled her fingers under the covers and waited grimly until the wind died down and the sense of a presence died with it. She checked the diamond ring to make sure it were still on her finger. Then she went to sleep.

It was the breeze that woke Mary the second night after the burial. Outside in the hall, a low groaning sound began: "Oooooooooo! Ooooooooo! Mary! Mary!"

A blue figure hovered in the doorway, changing shades rapidly from white-blue to sky blue to dark blue and back again, over and over. The strobing pattern made the shadows in the room flicker harshly, giving Mary a headache. She shuddered with chills and clutched the eiderdown close to her, the diamond ring sparkling in the changing blue light.

"Mary! I'm c-c-cold, Mary!" the ghost of Kate wailed despairingly.

"Why're you cold?" Mary retorted, closing her eyes against the flicker.

"The grave's so cold," the ghost wailed, making Mary shiver and shake under the eiderdown.

Mary shouted: "G'way ghost. G'way. I don't have nothing of yers."

The breeze swirled around her fer a minute or more, tugging at her hair, her face, her hands. She tucked the hand with the diamond ring under her armpit and grimly kept her eyes closed until the wind died down and the sense of a presence died with it. But she couldn't get back to sleep that night.

The next mornin', she visited one of the local conjure wimmen and asked how to get rid of a ghost. After she gave the conjurer a description of the ghost (though she dint tell her about the diamond ring), the woman done told her to ask the ghost to come into the room t'get warm. Mary nodded thoughtfully, Yes, maybe that would do the trick. Once Kate warmed up, she'd forget all about hauntin' her sister.

That night, when Mary felt the cold breeze begin to swirl through her room, she sat up in bed right away. Sure 'nuff, a glowing blue figure materialized in the doorway.

"Mary! I'm c-c-cold, Mary," the ghost of Kate wailed despairingly.

"Come on in then, ghost, and get you warm," Mary said, speaking as calmly as she could against the terrified lump in her throat. Her whole body was shaking like a tree in a windstorm as the blue figure floated closer and closer to the bed. It moved in a funny way, jerking this way and that like a puppet on a string. It seemed to be lookin' fer something. Mary's heart pounded s'hard her ribs hurt. She knew what the ghost were lookin' fer.

"Why'd ya come here, ghost?" she said, teeth chattering from fright.

"I'm looooookin' fer soooomethin'," the ghost wailed, jerking its glowing blue head back and forth.

"What you lookin' fer?" asked Mary. The guilty question slipped out of her mouth afore she could stop it.

"My riiiiiinnngg! I want my ring!" the ghost of Kate wailed, its voice rising s'high only hound dogs could hear the top notes. The pressure on Mary's ears was something awful. She clapped both hands over her ears and shouted: "I ain't got it!"

"Yes, you *do!*" roared the ghost.

Mary felt a wrenching pain in her hand, and then breeze, light, ghost, and sound vanished. Taking her hand and the diamond ring with it.

Mary fainted and dint wake up till morning. In the bright sunlight beaming onto her bed, she saw that her hand was gone! Only a black cauterized stump was left on the end of her arm.

Mary never explained to her daughters and nephew how she come to lose her hand. But she ain't never stole nothing again neither fer the rest of her days. She learned her lesson at last.

8

The Handshake

Polly was the sweetest, prettiest girl in Goldsboro, yes sir. All the local boys were chasing her, and quite a number of the fellows from the surrounding countryside were too. All the girls were jealous of Polly 'cause they didn't have no sweethearts to take them to the local dances, but even they couldn't help liking her. Polly would give someone the shirt off her back if they needed it. That's just the way she was. Of course, the girls all wanted Polly to choose her man so things could go back to normal. But Polly was picky. None of the local boys suited her, and neither did the fellows from the backcountry.

Then one day, George Dean came home from university, and Polly was smitten. He was handsome, tall, and mysterious. He didn't chase her like the other fellows. He seemed to favor the other girls. For weeks Polly fumed as George played beau to first one pretty girl then another. Didn't he see her at all? She was in a real tizzy by the time handsome George Dean wandered up to her front porch one evening and asked if she'd care to take a stroll down the lane. Polly sniffed and acted haughty at first, but finally she allowed that a stroll might not come amiss.

45

From that moment on, Polly and George were inseparable. You couldn't turn around without bumping into them at one social event or another. Polly completely dropped all her other beaus, much to the relief of the local girls, and soon the town was filled with the laughter of many courting couples. The Saturday night dances were particularly popular, and it was at one of those that George proposed and Polly accepted. There was great rejoicing— particularly among the eligible young females, who'd been afeared of what might happen if Polly broke it off with George.

A day was set, and Polly started making preparations for the wedding and shopping for items to fill her new home. George wasn't too interested in all the fripperies and wedding details. He left the womenfolk to get on with it and started spending time down at the pool hall with some of his buddies. And that's where he met Helene, the owner's saucy daughter. She had bold black eyes and ruby-red lips, and a bad-girl air that fascinated George. He spent more and more time at the pool hall, and less and less time with Polly, who finally noticed in spite of all the hustle and bustle.

She made a few inquiries, and Cindy—a girl who'd lost her favorite beau to Polly a few years back—told her *all about* Helene. In detail.

Of course, Polly was furious. She immediately confronted George with the story, and he couldn't deny it. Suddenly, George had to toe the mark. His pool-hall visits were over, and he spent every free hour he wasn't at work by her side. That didn't sit well with George, but his family backed Polly up, so he went along with it.

The day of the wedding dawned clear and bright. Polly and her bridesmaids went to the church to get dressed in their finery, whispering excitedly together. The guests filled the sanctuary, and the pastor and the best man waited patiently in the antechamber for the groom's arrival. They waited. And waited. And waited some more. But George didn't come.

The best man hurried into the sanctuary to talk to the groom's father, who hustled back to the house right quick to check on his son. Still no George. Had he been in an accident? Was he hurt? No one knew the answer.

George's brothers went searching for him, calling in at the police, at the hospital. His youngest brother even went to the pool hall. And that's when he found out that Helene was missing too. Helene's youngest sister told George's youngest brother that she'd seen them leave the pool hall together about an hour before the wedding. So that was that.

With dread, Polly's mother went to tell her daughter what had happened. Polly, all bright and shining and lovely in her long white dress and soft wedding veil, turned pale when her mother broke the news.

"It couldn't be. George would never do that!" she exclaimed. She stared blankly at her mother, swayed a bit, and then stiffened, grabbing her left arm as a sudden pain ripped through it. She was dead from a massive heart attack before she hit the floor.

And so Polly's wedding became—in essence—Polly's wake. Her family was furious. George's family was furious and embarrassed. And the guests were furious too. George's unthinking actions had killed the sweetest, prettiest girl in Goldsboro. If he was going to jilt her, the gossips all agreed, he should have done it privately. He shouldn't have left her at the altar.

A few days later Polly was buried in the churchyard, still wearing her white wedding dress and veil. The whole town came to the funeral and wept at the passing of such a beautiful young girl. George and Helene, who had spent the week happily honeymooning in the Outer Banks, arrived home at the very moment that the black-clad crowd exited the churchyard. Their arrival caused a commotion. The minister had to pull Polly's father off George before he killed him. And George's family disowned him right there in the street in front of everyone. Even the attorneys at the law office where George worked turned him away, knowing that no one in town would do business with them as long as George remained on their staff.

Helene's family was equally embarrassed. No one was visiting the pool hall anymore, and it looked like they would have to move away from town. They refused to open their door to their daughter and her new husband. Only Helene's youngest sister relented enough to open the upper window of the pool hall and speak to her sister. She dropped a bundle of clothes down to Helene and then slammed the window shut immediately afterward to make her position clear. So George and Helene left town in disgrace to make a new life for themselves elsewhere.

Life moved on. The scandal grew cold, and new ones took its place as new interests arose among the young people and the gossips. Polly and George and Helene were forgotten. Then, a year after Polly's death, George's father passed and was buried in the local churchyard just a few plots away from the girl who had almost become his daughter-in-law. This event triggered gossip about the fatal wedding day. For a few days the story of Polly and George was revived and much discussed.

Everyone in town turned out for the funeral of the elder Mr. Dean. Everyone was waiting to see if George would show his face. But George was too clever for them. He waited at an inn outside of town until it was dark, and then he went to the churchyard to pay his last respects to his father.

George Junior stood by the freshly dug grave and told his father that things weren't going so well. His old law firm had refused to give him a reference, and word of Polly's death had reached those at his former university who might have once helped him. So he was working as a farmhand, barely able to feed and clothe himself and his wife, who flagrantly chased after other men.

As he unburdened himself at his father's graveside, George heard a sweet female voice calling his name. "George. Sweetheart." George looked up in sudden hope. Was that his mother, come to forgive him? But no, the voice was pitched too high to be his mother, who sang contralto in the church choir.

"George," the voice called again. Puzzled, George turned toward the sound. And then he saw, rising up from a grassy mound under a spreading oak tree, a figure in a long white gown and a soft veil. Her eyes and her lips were yellow flames beneath the veil, and the rotted wedding dress glowed with a white yellow light. It was Polly.

George's body stiffened, shudders of fear coursing up and down his arms and legs. Every hair on his neck prickled, and bile rose up into his throat until he retched and threw up on his father's grave. He put a shaking hand to his mouth and staggered backward, the other hand outstretched to ward off the specter floating toward him.

THE HANDSHAKE

The spectral bride cackled with angry laughter and swooped forward until her hand closed over George's outstretched one in a terrible parody of a handshake. The grip of the spectral bride was so cold that it burned the skin, and so hard that the bones crunched as she squeezed. "Come along into the church, George," the glowing bride whispered. Through the veil, George could see maggots crawling in and out of Polly's flaming eye sockets.

"Nooo! Polly, no!" George screamed in terror, but he could not wrench his hand free. The ghost dragged him step by halting step toward the front door of the church. His hand was a red-hot agony of pain, though the rest of his body was shaking with cold. The agony was spreading now, up his arm to his shoulder.

"No!" George gave a final cry of despair and wrenched again at his hand. And suddenly, he was free. The spectral bride gave a roar of rage as George ran pell-mell down the church lane and out into the street.

"You're mine, George Dean! If not in this world, then in the next," the spectral bride howled after him. Her glowing form swelled upward until it was taller than the treetops. George looked back once and fell headlong when he saw the massive form with its flaming yellow eyes and lips and the moldering rags of its white wedding dress. He picked himself up, terror lending him speed. Clutching his aching hand, he ran all the way back to the inn.

By the time George reached his room, the fiery pain in his hand and arm was seeping through his entire body. He rang desperately for the housemaid and begged her to send for a doctor. Then he fell into bed and stared at his hand, which was black and withered, as if it had been scorched long ago by a fire. Black and red streaks were climbing up his arm so fast that he could almost see them move.

George was unconscious when the doctor arrived, and the swelling was already extending into his chest and neck. There was nothing the physician could do. The injury was too severe and had spread too far. Within two days George was dead. Polly had gotten her man at last.

9

Robah

When my boyfriend Fred and our friends Mike and Carrie suggested partying in the graveyard one Halloween night, I said, "Why not?" That seemed a suitably spooky thing to do. It was a cloudy night, with a great deal of wind rustling and shrieking through the trees. The wind whipped leaves and debris through the air, and great blasts of it would rattle the gravestones, which made me and Carrie shriek even worse than the wind. I wasn't really scared. What I really wanted was to have Fred put his arm around me, and by golly, it worked! Fred got all manly and protective, saying that no ghost dared mess with his girl while he was around.

"You hear me, ghosts!" he called aloud. "Don't mess with my girl!"

I lapped it up, snuggling contentedly against his side. But our friend Mike was dubious.

"I wouldn't say things like that in a graveyard," he said to Fred, shaking his head in the beam of the flashlight. "That's asking for trouble."

"Don't be silly. And come sit down here under this big gravestone," his girlfriend Carrie called to us. "It's kind of cozy in this spot, and it's out of the wind."

ROBAH

We looked around and saw that she'd put a blanket down on the ground by a big headstone and was busy pulling a bottle of wine from her backpack. We hurried over and settled cozily onto the blanket. It was almost like a picnic. Well, okay—make that a grisly picnic under a lowering black sky with a fierce wind whipping debris all over the place and hulking black tombstones all around us. The only light came from our flashlights, but it didn't help at all. There was some quality about the darkness that Halloween night that swallowed all the light.

As we sat in the hollow of the hill with a few icy fingers of wind creeping over us from time to time, I finally caught my breath and had a good look around. My eyes were adjusted to the darkness, and I could see a lot more than I expected. Row upon row of tombstones lined the rolling hillside. The shapes were strange sometimes, with statues and carvings interrupting the regularity of the headstones. Here and there a tree whipped wildly in that wind. It was almost gale force in its intensity, and something about its single-minded force made me shiver. For the first time that evening, I realized how truly creepy this place was. But there was no way I would admit that to anyone. Carrie was cheerfully passing out glasses of wine, and the boys were laughing.

I accepted a glass of wine from Carrie, and in the light of the flashlight, I read the name on the tombstone behind her: "Robah Gray."

Carrie blinked at me. "What?" she asked. Then she followed my gaze to the tombstone and grinned. "Oh. How thoughtless of me. Do you mind if we sit here, Robah?" she asked politely. There was (thank goodness) no response. The boys chuckled. Fred lifted the wine bottle and asked: "Want some wine, Robah?"

Still no answer (thank God).

I decided to concentrate on the wine and the conversation and to stop looking at the windswept graveyard around me. It was freaking me out. When I tuned in again, I realized Mike was still addressing the tombstone: "Don't you get tired of being stuck in this graveyard, Robah? I would." He drank the last of his wine and gestured for Fred to give him a refill. Only a few drops came out of the bottle.

"Wow. That went fast," said Carrie.

"We should have brought two bottles," said Mike with a sigh of regret.

I shivered as a few more fingers of wind found us around Robah's grave. Fred rubbed my shoulders and arms briskly to warm them and dropped a kiss on my hair.

"Annie's freezing," he announced. "We'd better get moving before she turns into an icicle."

Carrie and Mike jumped up at once, grabbing the empty bottle and blanket so quickly that I realized I wasn't the only one made uneasy by our eerie location.

"Thanks for sharing your spot with us, Robah," I said quietly to the tombstone, feeling that it wasn't respectful to leave without some acknowledgment. Silly, I know. But that's how I felt.

"Why don't you come along with us, Robah?" added Fred jovially, flinging his arm around my shoulders. "It would be more interesting than staying in a graveyard."

"Hush, Fred," I said uneasily.

I could see Mike's and Carrie's flashlights bobbing along as they navigated their way through the headstones. They were already halfway up the hillside and hurrying toward the car as fast as they could without running.

"Come on," I said, pulling Fred away as he continued to babble nonsense to Robah's grave. A great gust of wind followed us up the hillside, nearly knocking me off my feet. Fred's hand on my arm was the only thing that saved me from a nasty fall.

We reached the car only a step or two behind Carrie and Mike, and another great gust of wind blew right into the car with us.

"Whew. Creepy!" Carrie said, glancing over the front seat to where Fred and I huddled together in back.

"What a great Halloween!" Fred said cheerfully, squeezing my hand and smiling at me. Personally, I'd have preferred to go to a party. But when Fred smiled at me like that, I lost all desire to be anywhere else. I smiled back at him and then laid my head on his shoulder and fell asleep.

It was late by the time they dropped me off at my house. The wind was still gusting something fierce in the pine trees beside the house, and I seemed to be accompanied inside by a miniature whirlwind that tugged at my coat and scarf and nearly knocked me off my feet. I staggered and then shut the door on the wind, which continued to whistle around me for a moment even after the door was closed. Then I went into the den to sit for a moment beside the embers still glowing in the fireplace. I took off my hat and coat with a sigh of relief, happy to be home.

For some reason I thought of poor Robah, lying under the cold earth in the graveyard. I bet he—or was it she?—would like to be here right now! The thought made me shiver, in spite of the warmth from the fire. And when the wind gusted against the window so fiercely that the pane shook, I jumped and whirled in fright.

Enough was enough, I scolded myself, and went upstairs to bed. I was done with creepy things for one night. Well, not quite. The TV in the family room turned itself on in the middle of the night at top volume. Scared the whole family. Dad was furious—thought it was me playing tricks. But I was sleeping in my bed when it happened. Pretty strange.

As soon as I stepped into the den after my college classes the next day, the knocking began. It sounded like someone was striking the floorboards with a hammer. Except there's only a narrow crawl space under the floor of our den, and that's boarded up. I stared around the room, looking for an explanation while the pounding rattled the floorboard. The howling wind from the graveyard had died away to nothing— and there were no trees beside the house on that side. Blast. No explanation there.

Then the hammering noise stopped abruptly, and the room became unnaturally still. And I *felt* someone in there with me. Staring at me. Okay—that was too creepy for me. My backpack fell from my nerveless fingers as I backed out of the den. I bolted into the kitchen to ask my mother about the knocking noise. Loud as it had seemed in the den, Mom hadn't heard it in the kitchen. Double weird.

I had a lump in my throat the size of Texas when I crept down the hall to retrieve my backpack from the den. Was the invisible person still there? The room seemed empty. As I stepped inside, the TV turned on all by itself and started flipping wildly through the channels. The pounding of my heart was echoed by a throbbing in my temples as I dove forward, grabbed my backpack, and ran for the stairs. As soon as my sneakers hit the hallway, the TV turned off. Oh boy!

I went up to my room and called Fred. My hands were shaking so much I could hardly dial. "I think my den is haunted," I told him.

"Say again?" Fred said, bemused. I told him about the TV and about the knocking and about the invisible presence I felt in the den.

"Do you think Robah followed me home?" I asked nervously.

"Don't be silly," said Fred. But his voice had a note of uncertainty that I did not find comforting.

I did my homework in my room and didn't come down until Mom called me to supper. After washing up the dishes, I reluctantly joined my parents in the den, carrying a big bowl of popcorn. The fire was dancing merrily in the grate; the TV was burbling out a game show; Mom was piecing a quilt. Everything was normal. Relieved, I sat down on the loveseat with a book. And an invisible someone sat down next to me with a sigh of contentment.

I leapt so high that my bottom actually left the seat, and popcorn spilled everywhere. My parents gave me an odd look. "Be careful, Annie," Dad said from the recliner. Hastily, I handed the bowl of popcorn to my mom and crawled around on the floor, picking up popcorn and carefully avoiding the invisible person on the loveseat. Oddly, there was a person-size shape on the loveseat that was completely free of spilled popcorn. As I stared at it, a single kernel on top of the loveseat floated up into the air, as if it had been plucked up by an invisible hand, and then disappeared in midair as if it had been popped into an invisible mouth.

Grabbing the last pieces of popcorn from the rug, I dumped them into the trash can and said, "I've got to finish my homework." Then I ran for the door. I heard Mom say,

"Annie's acting very strange tonight," and Dad replied, "Kids!" Then I slammed shut the door of my room against invisible entities that ate popcorn. I called Fred. There was no way I was going to share my den with a ghost!

It turned out Fred was playing in a football game the following night, but he was free Friday evening. So I invited him to come to dinner with the family, and then we could do some ghost busting in the den while my parents went next door for their weekly game of bridge with the neighbors. Fred agreed.

I had trouble going to sleep that night, afraid the ghost would not confine its activities to the den. But aside from the sounds of late-night television coming from downstairs around 2:00 a.m.—softer this time so it wouldn't wake my parents—I didn't hear from the ghost again until the following afternoon. I was hovering in the hallway, holding a bag of potato chips and a soda, wondering if I should have my snack in the den with the ghost or eat it upstairs. Then the phone rang in the den. I went to answer it, dropping the open bag of chips and the can of soda onto the end table beside the loveseat.

The caller asked for my mom, so I ran to the kitchen to get her. As I left the room, I heard a loud crash. I hastened down the hall and stuck my head into the kitchen to tell Mom to pick up the phone extension by the refrigerator. Then, morbid with curiosity, I went back to the den to see what the invisible person had done this time. I found soda dripping down the wall of the den, and the crumpled can lying on the floor in a puddle of soda and soggy potato chips.

My heart pounded so hard that I felt as if I'd been running a marathon. "Okay, no soda or potato chips," I said aloud. "Next time I'll make popcorn."

There came an enthusiastic knocking from the floorboards under my feet. I *really* didn't like it when the ghost answered me! I backed out hastily to get paper towels and a mop to clean up the mess before Mom saw it. I didn't want to drag my parents into this ghostly business.

The room was silent and watchful as I cleaned the soda from the wall and picked up the soggy chips. When I hurried away, I heard the TV turn on all by itself. I made out the faint sounds of a game show as I climbed the stairs to my room. Only one more day, I thought grimly as I settled at my desk to do my homework. Then you're outta here, my ghostly friend!

Fred showed up promptly at 6:00 p.m. for dinner the next night. My parents were glad to see him. They liked Fred and approved of our relationship. When dinner was finished, my parents went next door to play their weekly game of bridge with the neighbors. They invited Fred and me, but we said we'd rather watch TV in the den.

As soon as they were gone, I dragged Fred down the hall. The moment he stepped foot in the den, the knocking began. Thud, thud, thud went the floorboards. Then the TV turned on and began roaming wildly from channel to channel. The lights flickered like strobes in a dance club.

"It's good to see you too, Robah," Fred shouted loudly. Immediately, the lights stopped flickering, the pounding stopped, and the TV settled itself onto another game show. Apparently, Robah was addicted to them.

Fred patted my hand reassuringly and then said aloud, "Thanks so much for coming to visit, Robah. But it's time to go home now."

Silence, save for the smarmy voice of the game-show host blaring from the TV.

"Come on out to the car, Robah," Fred said. He walked to the front door and shrugged into his coat, beckoning for me (and Robah) to follow him. So I did, putting on coat and scarf against the chilly autumn air. But the TV stayed on in the den.

We walked out to the car and got inside. Then we got back out, went back into the house, and stood in the doorway of the den. "Come on out to the car, Robah," Fred said again, very gently. "Time to go home."

He turned and walked back outside. Hesitantly, I followed him. This time, I heard the TV turn off, and a miniature whirlwind accompanied me to the car, tugging at my coat and scarf as I walked.

We drove to the graveyard in silence and parked in the same place we'd parked on Halloween. "Come on, Robah. We're almost home," said Fred to the empty backseat as we got out of the car. We held hands as we walked slowly down the hill to the tombstone where we'd had our alfresco picnic. A small breeze accompanied us down the slope, whistling through my hair and brushing gently against my cheek. When we reached the grave site, the wind grew fierce and strong, whirling around us and blowing dead leaves into the air. "Welcome home, Robah," I said, my voice steady despite my jangled nerves.

We waited for the breeze to die down before we went back to the car.

"Do you think it worked?" I asked Fred as we drove away.

"Only one way to find out," he said, and he took us back to my house. The den, when we entered, was blessedly silent and free of invisible presences. Our cans of soda and the big bag of potato chips we brought in with us remained untouched. And we had to turn on the TV when we wanted to see a program. It was a real relief.

"Guess Robah is gone," I said, reaching over to give Fred's hand a grateful squeeze.

"Looks like it," he said laconically. He brushed his fingers lightly against my cheek and added: "I think next year, we should go to a Halloween party. I've had enough of graveyards!"

"Me too," I nodded emphatically. "Me too!"

10

Busted!

It was the opportunity of a lifetime. That's what Abel said. Of course, that's what Abel always said when we started a new scam. But this time, it looked like he was right. Ghost busting was the way to go, Abel said. So that was the way we went.

We needed props to make us look convincing to potential customers, so we purchased secondhand robes of a standard variety to make us look ministerial. Jacob brought along his humongous old family Bible—the kind that took two hands to lift. And I supplied several handbells thoughtfully swiped from a set when the local church lost funding from the diocese and had to shut its doors. Armed with these, a gross of white candles, and other sacred objects of the "trade," we started our new career in ghost busting.

We'd lurk in the local bars downtown and spot older citizens of a more superstitious variety. Blatant eavesdropping on the tipsy produced a few leads, and a week after our initial investment in tools, we were at the house of a little old lady called Wanda, graciously accepting tea and biscuits and hearing all about the "banging in the attic" caused by her ghost. It kept her up at night. She was always nervous. Sometimes she heard footsteps overhead. This was, Abel assured Wanda, typical ghostly behavior, and it was a good thing she'd called us to come lay the spirit to rest.

In my opinion, the show we put on was worth every penny of the exorbitant fee we charged old lady Wanda out of her retirement fund. All three of us put on robes with miters, and Abel had given me a fancy crosier he had picked up at a costume store. We staked out the attic, making a huge circle of white candles, dripping "holy water" in every corner, on every window, and all over the door. Jacob stood in the center of the candle ring holding the huge Bible and looking suitably pious. I stood beside him holding one large handbell that struck a doleful note that reverberated through the boards of the dusty attic.

Since I was the only one who had studied Latin, it was my job to do the chanting. Abel "translated" the proceedings to Wanda as we proceeded with the ceremony. My favorite moment was when Jacob's face creased with horror and he staggered backward, holding up the Bible defensively toward the "phantom of the attic." I struck a valiant pose, rang the bell rapidly several times, and threw holy water over the "ghost."

"Hallelujah! Thank you, God!" Abel shouted from his observer's position. He pumped Wanda's hand enthusiastically. "Your ghost is gone, ma'am," he told her as we sagged dramatically with relief before straightening our shoulders and cleaning up the candle ring. Wanda told us we were fine boys and wrote us a large check from her pension. Better yet, she said she'd recommend us to all her friends. Our first endorsement!

"Any banging you hear up here now is just that large branch outside your windowpane," Abel told her, leading her to the

BUSTED!

window to show her the tall oak planted too close to the house. "Any footsteps are squirrels. Your ghost is gone!"

Wanda was as good as her word. Calls started pouring in. Mostly older folks with creaky houses and time on their hands. Oh, and we had one gig where we removed a "weeping baby" from a house shared by six pretty girls just out of college. Abel got a date out of that gig while Jacob and I got bitten by the raccoon we found living in their garage. We had to get rabies shots too, which really made us mad.

"Next time, *you're* carrying that heavy Bible, and I'm holding the hand of the pretty girl," Jacob told Abel sharply. I stood in the background looking noncommittal and refrained from mentioning the visit I'd paid the girls the next day to show them the wounds the "ghost" had given me. After that visit, my dating calendar was booked solid through February!

By this time, we had more than a hundred thousand dollars in the bank, and we were sitting pretty. Everyone was happy with our "services," and the cops hadn't heard a word about us—a state of affairs that was unusual for us at this stage of the game.

Our next gig was more than an hour outside the city, deep into the Smokies. It was an old Victorian monstrosity that must have been inspired by Asheville's Biltmore House, because it was constructed on a similar—if ever so slightly smaller—scale. We turned into a ragged, overgrown driveway at dusk, and our headlights picked out the looming atrocity with its saggy old porch, cracked windowpanes, peeling paint, and rotting roof.

"Are you sure we've got the right address?" Jacob asked nervously as I navigated the car over the ruts in the gravel driveway.

"This is the place," Abel said confidently from the backseat, where he sat by the huge Bible and box of candles. "They are going to pay us fifty thousand smackeroos to get rid of their ghost! That's half again what we've already earned so far from this gig. Makes you wish you'd really gone into the priesthood."

"Or not," I said sarcastically, thinking of my pleasantly full date book.

"See, here comes our host for the evening," Abel said, pointing to a hunched figure coming down the warped front steps.

"His name isn't Igor, is it?" asked Jacob, his eyes popping. I understood exactly what he meant. The hunched white-haired fellow looked as if he was the assistant of mad Dr. Jekyll or perhaps Dr. Frankenstein himself.

"We didn't prepare for vampires," I joked nervously as the old man walked up to the door of the car.

"Will you two shut up!" Abel growled from the backseat. He threw on his "best customer" smile and leapt out of the car to greet the old man. Now that the man was visible in the headlights, I saw that the "hunch" was made by a shotgun cradled on his right arm. The man had a long, flowing beard, a gnarled old face, and the meanest black eyes you've ever seen. Oh boy! This was a real mountain man! Forget about monsters. This old fellow looked hard enough to chase us all the way to China if we didn't deliver good service tonight.

"We've got a real mean ghost tonight, boys," Abel said as we decamped from the car and began gathering our paraphernalia from the backseat. "Mr. Hatfield here says it's a screaming head. Isn't that right, Amos?"

"S'right," said the tough little man, glaring at us and fingering his shotgun thoughtfully. "'Pears on top of the main staircase and comes rolling down in flames, screaming all the way."

"Sounds ghastly," Abel said cheerfully. "But we'll soon put it to rights. Come on, fellows, let's set up in the hallway."

The inside of the house was just as warped and creepy as the outside. Cobwebs festooned the walls and ceiling. The rooms were chilly and smelled of dust and mildew. Old sheets—once white but now gray with dust—covered all the furniture, making everything look ghostly. I swear there was even one portrait on the wall of the hallway that had eyes that moved!

"Can't rent out the place," the old man said defensively when he saw my disapproving stare at all the dust piled everywhere. "Folks are too plumb scared of the haint. N'point in keeping it clean if I can't rent it. You boys set it right fer me, and I'll keep you in business 'til it's time to retire!"

Out of the corner of my eye, I saw Abel rub his hands together in glee at the notion. Personally, I wasn't so sure. Of course, I didn't believe in ghosts myself. But if anyplace was haunted, this would be the place!

The staircase dominated the front foyer. It was wide enough to belong in Biltmore House and ran upward for twenty-five steps before disappearing into the upper story. It had a lovely oak railing, and the wall beside it featured portraits of stern-faced ancestral types. Near the bottom was a small landing, with two stairs angling off to the right to complete the bottom of an "L." A dreadful flowered runner in a faded red went up the center of the stairs, pooled on the landing, and then continued upward past the old folks in the portraits. Someone needed to do some serious redecorating of this house once we got it "busted."

We set up our candle circle just in front of the wooden archway that framed the staircase. I lit about fifty candles while Jacob sloshed "holy" water up and down the staircase and in the corners of the room, soaking his ceremonial black robes. Somehow, Abel wriggled out of carrying the heavy Bible—again—and stood by the front door with old man Amos as I straightened the miter on my head. I nodded once to Jacob, staggering already under the weight of the massive tome, stepped into the candle circle with my crosier and handbell, and began a long chant in completely nonsensical Latin. I'd had a lot of practice lately and sounded magnificent as I droned my way up and down the scale, punctuating the sentences with mournful tolls of the bell.

I was about three-quarters of the way through my chant and was preparing to gesture with my crosier toward the "phantom" of the house, when the laughter began. It was a supernatural sound that reached inside my body and triggered every nerve ending. It had a strange echo as if the voice were laughing inside a dark cavern. I exchanged alarmed glances with Jacob as the laugh grew louder, and I sneaked a look over my shoulder at Abel, who was several shades paler than he'd been a moment before.

Then, in a tone of doom, the voice spoke.

"I come!" it cried. "I come!"

"I go! I go!" Jacob gasped beside me, nearly on his knees under the weight of the heavy Bible.

"Don't talk nonsense, man. And stand up straight!" I snapped over the heavy beating of my heart. My skin felt clammy and cold, and sweat was trickling down my forehead and across my neck.

A green light sprang up at the top of the staircase. It hovered there for a moment and then started to spin itself into a face. It was a monster face—like a Gorgon. Wild hair streamed everywhere, and sharp teeth jutted up from the wide lips. The nose was twisted and broken, and the eyes were glowing with red flames. It opened its mouth and started to scream—a horrible loud shriek that made every hair on my body stand on end. Then it burst into flames and rolled straight down the staircase toward us, making the turn at the end with the grace born of long experience. It headed right toward the candle ring!

I dropped the handbell and leapt backward, holding the crosier in front of me for protection. Unfortunately, my robes went right through the candle flames and caught fire. I staggered backward toward the door, slapping at the flames, unable to tear my horrified gaze from the approaching phantom. Its green head blazed with phantom red flames, and its scream made me want to wriggle right out of my crawling skin.

Jacob was facedown in the center of the candle ring, the Bible held over his head when the phantom reached him. To my horror, I saw him rise up—Bible and all—as if he were carried on a massive wind. Then he was tossed right past me through one of the wide windows framing the door. Jacob gave a shout of terror as glass shattered everywhere. Abel and I were littered with the shards, and tiny red cuts covered my face and hands.

I noticed peripherally that Amos seemed to have disappeared from the hallway, but that was all I had time to note before the head came for me. Abel was struggling desperately with the latch on the front door as the phantom wind wrapped around me with the force of a giant's fist. I was sent flying upward right through the ceiling. Plaster and boards and jagged ends of wood cascaded around me. I would have been knocked out if I hadn't had the miter on my head. I was lifted so high that my head hit the ceiling of the third story before the phantom fist dropped me onto the second-story floor. Somehow, I rolled onto my feet and dove straight for the front window. Thankfully, my subconscious had remembered there was a front porch. I fell only a few feet before I hit the rotting roof of the porch and crashed through it, down onto the glass-strewn boards below.

Inside the house I heard Abel screaming. The front door burst open beside me, and Abel staggered backward through it, covered in glowing green flames. The bodiless head was laughing again, and it was three times the size it had been when it first appeared. I leapt to my feet, grabbed Abel by the flaming arm—a heroic act on my part—and hustled him off the porch into the yard. Jacob was in the car already, frantically trying to turn around in the narrow driveway. We approached the car at a run. I wrenched open the door and flung Abel and myself into the backseat.

Fortunately for all, the green flames covering Abel extinguished as soon as we entered the vehicle. Jacob gunned the motor, and we raced out of the driveway and down the hill with such speed that the wheels of the car sometimes left the ground on the tighter curves. None of us spoke. We were shaking with reaction, and all of us were bleeding from the cuts we'd received when the window broke. Plus I had a huge bump on my head where it had crashed through the ceiling.

Jacob didn't slow the car until we reached the outskirts of Asheville. "I don't know about you two, but my ghost-busting days are over," he announced as we entered the city. Abel and I heartily concurred.

I found out later that Abel had gotten tipsy when he went out with the pretty girl from the crying-baby house and had let it slip that a raccoon—not a ghost—had inflicted those wounds on Jacob and me. Since her family ran an illegal moonshine business on the side, she didn't want to go to the police about our little scam. So she asked her Uncle Amos to introduce us to a real ghost to pay us back for our little deception. So in the end, we were the ones who got busted!

The Rescue

WILMINGTON

That stormy night in the winter of 1897 was undoubtedly the strangest and most terrifying evening I've ever spent on the river. At the time, I was captain of a steamer and ran a ferry service out of Wilmington. On the night in question, we were bound for Southport. Heavy sleet was thundering down on the ship, it was pitch dark, and ice was floating on the river. It made for a difficult run. Frankly, I was steering more by instinct and the memory of hundreds of previous trips, rather than by sight.

Our only passenger stayed up top in the pilothouse with me, keeping warm and dry and entertaining me with sea stories. He was an elderly man from Scotland, and I quite liked him in spite of his tendency to ramble. There was a twinkle in his eyes that bespoke a good heart.

As we made slow progress toward Southport, he related a story about one of his ancestors who had come to America just before the Revolutionary War. Having distinguished himself at the Battle of Culloden in the Highlands, this illustrious ancestor was invited to join the Scottish settlement in Cape Fear by no less a personage than colonial governor Gabriel Johnson. The Highland Scot took to his new home with enthusiasm, and when the American Revolution came, he sided with the rebels.

The Highlander's activities did not go unnoticed by the British troops stationed at Wilmington. He was captured along with two other Whigs and imprisoned in the hull of a prison ship in the harbor to await his death. At the appointed hour, the three manacled men were placed onto an old barge and poled out to a place near the ruins of Governor Tryon's palace. They stood trial there and were sentenced to death. The two Whigs were led out first, bound to a large tree, and then shot to death by a firing squad. The Highlander was then brought forth and released from his shackles, preparatory to binding him to the same tree where the Whigs had just perished. For a single moment, the Highlander was free and unbound. And in that moment, he sprang forth, knocking his guards aside and running away into the forest. The British soldiers followed immediately, but the Highlander was too quick for them. He evaded recapture and eventually made his way home safely, just as the war ended and the British left the South for good. "He was lucky," I said to fill the pause that followed. Another lash of sleet hit the window of the pilothouse. I peered fruitlessly into the darkness ahead, hoping I was still on course.

"Very lucky," the passenger said. "He lived out the full length of his days and died in 1800. The other Whigs weren't so lucky." He paused for a moment and glanced sideways at me as if to gauge my reaction to his next remark. Then he said, "On stormy nights, the ghosts of the manacled Scotsmen are sometimes seen floating on a barge in the port near Brunswick. Perhaps they are reliving their final moments, hoping for a better ending?"

A huge gust of wind slammed against the pilothouse, rattling the windows and driving sleet sharply against the roof. I shuddered a bit, remembering the whispers I'd heard up and down the river about the ghostly barge seen floating in the harbor. At least now I knew the story behind the spirits.

The storm was growing worse, and conversation lagged as my attention was needed for the tricky piloting. I was afraid we would founder as the storm worsened, becoming in ferocity as strong as a hurricane. My crew were taking soundings constantly, trying to keep us in the channel. Then one of the deckhands burst into the pilothouse, shouting that we had lost the channel and were drifting toward some jetties. The next moment, the steamer rattled from stem to stern, caught fast on an underwater jetty. I raced out into the storm, slipping and sliding on the sleet-covered deck. A quick assessment told me we were locked down until the turn of the tide, but otherwise the steamer was unharmed.

Since we had an hour or so before the turn of the tide, I ordered the crew belowdecks to stay warm and dry in the furnace room, leaving only the first mate on duty outside. Then I returned to the pilothouse to keep my solo passenger company while we waited. About fifteen minutes after the accident, Jorgenson, the mate working the decks, came sliding into the pilothouse, white as a sheet, ice crystals shimmering on the ends of his hair.

"Sir! I saw . . . I saw . . ." Jorgenson's face contorted, and he stopped abruptly, shaking from head to toe. In his agitation, he dropped the lantern he was holding onto the floor.

"Calm down, man," I barked. "What did you see?"

Jorgenson rubbed his face with shaking hands. "There was a man," he began again. "I saw a bearded man in rough, tattered clothes appear suddenly by the rail, clutching at it as if it were a lifeline, and his face was . . ." Jorgenson shuddered and changed course in mid-sentence. "Well, let's just say he was terrified. He pointed out into the storm with his left hand. I ran over to help him, but when I grabbed at his arm to help him aboard, he . . . vanished!"

The passenger and I both exclaimed in disbelief.

"You've had too much to drink," I said, shaking my head. But Jorgenson insisted it was true. So I swept the lantern from where it lay on the floor, shrugged into my wet-weather gear, and made a search of the deck. The Scottish passenger helped me search, but Jorgenson refused to leave the refuge of the pilothouse. Of course, we found nothing but icy decks, pouring sleet, and howling rain.

Jorgenson still looked a little green when we got back to the pilothouse. I poured all of us a drink while I related the results of our search. The mate insisted that he had seen a phantom at the rail.

"The lantern light struck him full in the face," Jorgenson said. "I couldn't have been mistaken."

Agreeing to disagree, we waited another forty-five minutes for the turning tide and the steady rotation of the propellers to shift us off the underwater jetty. Then we were back in the channel and on our way down the stormy river, rolling in the heavy waves but moving steadily forward.

As I navigated cautiously through the maelstrom, a storm-tossed gull slammed suddenly into the window of the pilothouse, smashing the glass and landing at the feet of our Scottish passenger.

"A bad omen," he gasped, staring down at the panting, bleeding gull lying at his feet. Icy air filled the pilothouse, and

I stared from the passenger's white face to Jorgenson's shaking hands.

"'Tis a ghostly night, surely. But not all omens are bad," I said finally, to lighten the mood. "Put the poor creature somewhere warm until it recovers. And Jorgenson, why don't you set up an extra watch, just in case any more ghosts decide to appear for us tonight! If the crew are busy, they won't be so likely to panic if they see a phantom."

My jocular tone reassured the passenger and the mate. The passenger blocked up the broken pane as best he could while Jorgenson arranged for a special watch to give the nervous crew something useful to do.

As the crew moved briskly about the deck, I steered us carefully through the huge storm waves and falling ice. The wind shook the pilothouse again and again as our solo passenger mildly discussed other terrible storms he'd seen over the years. Various crew members, back on duty now that we were moving, came in and out of the pilothouse as they went about their allotted tasks, and everything seemed normal.

Then we heard a sharp human scream coming from the farther shore. It pierced even the fierce blowing of the wind and the sharp staccato of sleet on the roof. I jumped, and my hands started shaking on the wheel.

"By all that is holy! What was that?" gasped the passenger. The crew crowded into the pilothouse, exclaiming in confusion. The fear in the air was palpable now. To calm things down, I ordered a full stop. The engines cut out, and suddenly the sound of the storm was much louder. The ship started to roll as it settled into the trough of a large wave. And then, over the roar of the storm, the scream came again.

At that moment I realized where we were. The scream was coming from the direction of the old anchorage where the colonial prison ship once held three Highland Whigs waiting for death. Pulse pounding madly in my throat and wrists, I ordered all the crew to take special watches around the deck to see if we could spot the source of the scream. Sleet pummeled us as we strained our eyes in the wave-tossed darkness. Over the howling wind, the scream came a third time. And then we saw it.

Out in the darkness where the old ship had anchored, a dark object became visible through great sheets of rain and sleet. It glowed with a phosphorescent light, and in that light I saw an ancient rowing barge, slimy with seaweed and gnarled with barnacles. It looked as if it hadn't been used in a hundred years or more. It was a ghastly vision, and I was transfixed at the sight. My legs were shaking so badly that I could barely stand, but I kept my voice calm as I ordered the men to be ready to heave a line to the stricken vessel. They prepared to obey, straining eyes forward toward the ancient barge. By now we could make out two huge, gaunt figures in tattered Highland kilts standing on the barge. There were heavy chains around their legs and arms, and their wrists and ankles were raw and bleeding from the rubbing shackles. When they saw our steamer, both men reached forward as far as the chains would allow, beckoning us to their aid. I swallowed heavily, cleared my throat, and again ordered the mate to throw them a line.

Jorgenson, hands trembling visibly from the gruesome sight, heaved the line over the side. At that moment the barge and ship were both slammed by a huge storm wave. Everyone shouted and grabbed for a solid surface as water poured everywhere. The steamer rocked heavily and remained upright. But the barge was

THE RESCUE

swallowed up by the wave, and the line floated unclaimed in the water. We searched the dark, stormy waves with our lanterns, but the ghastly barge with its tattered prisoners had vanished as surely as Jorgenson's phantom.

Finally, I ordered the engines started, and we moved downriver in the direction of the floating barge, all hands keeping watch for the vanished vessel. Maybe the men we'd seen had been the Highland phantoms from our passenger's story, or maybe they weren't. I wasn't taking any chances, though. If injured or capsized men were out there, we would find them and bring them aboard.

After ten minutes of searching, one of the watchers gave a mighty shout. A wreck had been sighted. We changed course quickly to avoid crashing into the ship, which had gone bottom up. Through the howling wind and raging sleet, two figures could be discerned clinging to the overturned hull. We immediately came to the rescue, and soon both men had been brought aboard ship.

As the light of the lantern fell on the face of the first, Jorgenson gasped and grabbed hold of the wall in the pilothouse to steady himself. It was the bearded "phantom" who had appeared to him at the rail of the steamer earlier that evening! Furthermore, Jorgenson had seen the man pointing along the river in the direction where we'd found the wreck, which—coincidentally—was the same direction the Highlanders on the barge had been drifting when they beckoned for us to follow them.

The two men were all that remained of the seven-person crew of their ship. The other five crew members had been swept overboard during the storm and drowned. The two survivors had clung to the hull of the ship for hours, calling out over the storm as best they could while they gradually lost strength and their hope of rescue grew dim.

I piloted the steamer with its three passengers safely into Southport that night and waited out the storm before returning to Wilmington, which gave me plenty of time to mull over the events of that frightening evening. If we hadn't heard the phantom screaming and seen the glowing Highland barge, we would not have been watching the river for survivors and would have crashed right into the wrecked ship. And what of the man seen by Jorgenson clutching desperately to the rail of the steamer? Was it possible that the spirit of a man wrecked miles away could really span the distance between our ships to summon us to his rescue? It remains a mystery to this day.

12

Plucked

MURPHY

Hard times fell on the Mortimer family after the war. Penury forced them out of their home, and they moved into an old cabin at the outskirts of town to scratch what living they could from the land. The missus was a bitter woman by the time her man up and died, leaving her with two little boys to feed. She'd come from a wealthy family, but they'd thrown her out when she married, and they wouldn't take her back after her man passed.

The Mortimer boys were raised hard. Every attitude of their bitter, selfish, money-loving mother was embraced by them to the full. They looked down on their neighbors and picked fights with all the local children. When the oldest chap was twelve, they built a still up in the holler and started running moonshine across the state line to earn a little cash. When they couldn't sell shine, they went to the local school to cheat their school chums out of some cash. The brothers would set up card games, bully the other boys into playing, and then fleece their classmates of every penny. When the schoolboys protested, the eldest Mortimer made a great show of cleaning his gun while the younger Mortimer started sharpening his knife with a flint. The schoolboys got the hint and took off quick, leaving their money behind.

Drinking, hunting, quarreling, and swindling became a way of life for the Mortimer boys. So it shouldn't have come as a surprise when the missus got her finger shot off one day when she interfered in a quarrel between her two lads. They were having a shouting match over $4 that the younger Mortimer had borrowed from the elder and couldn't pay back. The shouting got so loud that it gave the missus a headache. So she marched out to the gate to give both her lads a licking. Unfortunately for her, that was the moment the elder Mortimer boy pulled out his gun. Unfortunately for him, the bullet meant to scare his brother into coughing up the cash not only took off his mama's middle finger but also entered the forehead of his baby brother, killing him instantly. But the judge was real understanding about it. After all, the younger Mortimer brother had pulled a knife on his brother. So the killing was ruled as self-defense.

"Served him right," the elder Mortimer muttered defensively to his mama, standing at the graveside of his younger brother. "He shouldn't a' borrowed the money if'n he couldn't pay it back."

What could the missus say to that? He was quoting the very words she'd used herself so many times, railing against the foolishness of her neighbors.

The elder Mortimer didn't want to admit that he missed his brother. Now there was no one to participate in his money-making schemes, no one to help with the still. Everyone in town was avoiding him, and the judge had told him straight out that if the elder Mortimer appeared in his courtroom again, he'd get twenty years in the slammer.

The night after the burial, the elder Mortimer boy had a strange dream. In his dream his younger brother came to him, white-faced and dead, with a red bullet hole in his forehead. He floated bonelessly up to the bed where the elder Mortimer lay, reached down with icy-cold fingers, and yanked a single strand from his brother's bushy red hair. It hurt like the dickens. The elder Mortimer let out a yell and woke himself up. His scalp was stinging where the ghost had touched it. When he rubbed it, a clump of hair fell out, plucked from his head by the roots.

"Maaa!" the elder Mortimer wailed in panic, rubbing at the bald spot on his head.

The missus came running, shocked to see her tough son wide-eyed as a frightened baby. She examined the small bald spot and firmly told him a mouse must have gotten into his bed and nibbled off his hair. The elder brother, shaking with cold, tried to believe her. But he couldn't figure out how a mouse could pluck hairs out by the roots.

The next night, almost as soon as he closed his eyes, the elder Mortimer boy saw his younger brother floating through the open window of the cabin. The dead boy's face was a hollow mask under the grotesque red hole in his forehead. His cheeks had withered overnight, collapsing inward like the cheeks of an ancient man, and his blue eyes were wide open and staring sightlessly at nothing. The elder Mortimer lay paralyzed with fright as the corpse drifted nearer, stretching out its hand toward his head. Cold fingers ran through his scalp and then yanked hard.

The elder Mortimer woke with a scream and sat up, huge chunks of hair scattering all over the bed and onto the floor— plucked out by the roots. The missus came running when she heard him, and she couldn't explain away the huge bald patch covering the right half of her boy's head, from his forehead all the way down to his neck.

PLUCKED

"I'm being hainted," the elder boy wailed, wringing his hands like a tiny child. "Make it stop, Mama! Make it stop!"

"I'll get a preacher-man to come pray over the cabin," the missus said. "That'll frighten away any haints, don't you worry."

The elder Mortimer brother was comforted by this plan, but he still sat up the rest of the night feeding the fire to keep the cabin nice and bright. At dawn he went up to the holler and spent the day making moonshine while his mama called the preacher-man out to exorcise the haint. But he was tired out after his long, sleepless night. He lay down by the still to get some rest.

And dreamed of his younger brother. The dead boy's skin was rotting away from his face and hands, revealing bone underneath his eyes and allowing his sagging nose to collapse inward. The red bullet hole gaped in his forehead, and his dead head lolled against his shoulder. His white hands, bones poking through his fingertips, stretched out toward his brother's hair and pulled . . .

The elder Mortimer boy screamed himself awake, hair showering all around him, spilling over the boards of the still and across the dirt floor. He clutched at his head, which was plucked bald. With a long, wordless wail, he ran down the hill and burst into the cabin, where the preacher-man was standing with his holy book and a goblet of holy water. The boy fell to his knees in front of the preacher-man.

"Make it stop! Make it stop!" he sobbed, his bald head pressed against the man's shiny black shoes.

Behind him, the door was caught by a huge blast of frigid air. The wind slammed the door so hard that it splintered and sagged on its hinges. Filling the doorway was a rotting corpse, maggots writhing in and out of its eye sockets, bones gaping through withered gray skin, head lolling against bare shoulder bones. Its forehead was dominated by a huge, bloodstained bullet hole. It staggered forward on bony legs, its withered hands reaching toward the elder Mortimer boy.

The preacher screamed. The missus screamed.

The skeleton's fingers closed on the scraggly beard growing from the boy's chin . . . and yanked.

The elder Mortimer boy convulsed once against the preacher's shiny black shoes. Then he rolled onto his back, mouth agape, eyes staring sightlessly up at the holy book and goblet still held in the minister's hands. Every single hair had been plucked from his body—arms, legs, face, hands, and torso. Small red hairs were slowly raining down onto the dirt floor of the cabin, covering every surface and sprinkling the heads of the preacher-man and the missus. A few hairs landed in the holy goblet.

The missus screamed and ran. She ran out of the house, out of the yard, out of the town, and kept running. She was never seen again. The preacher, made of sterner material, wiped the hair off his holy book, said a prayer over the plucked corpse of the elder Mortimer boy, and carried him back to the churchyard to be buried.

After the deaths of the two Mortimer brothers, no one would go near the haunted cabin just outside town. In a few seasons it rotted away until only a few boards and a broken-down chimney were left to show where it once stood.

As for the old still . . . Well, they say a feller out hunting whistle pigs a month after the Mortimer boy's death stumbled across the old still and helped himself to a whole jug full of moonshine. When he awoke the next morning, he was completely bald. After that, no one went near the old still or the holler it sat in neither, just in case!

PART TWO
Powers of Darkness and Light

Boo-Hag

ELIZABETH CITY

You know how they say some folks are lucky at cards and some are lucky at love? Well, that fit Bobby Hansen to a T. He was the best poker player in the county, but somehow he couldn't find himself a bride. Oh, he proposed to several girls and even got accepted by a few. But they always got cold feet a day or two before the wedding, and it was bye-bye Bobby.

After the third time, Bobby was mighty discouraged, and his pa felt real sore for him. They worked together in the family grocery store, and Bobby would sometimes sit on top of the pickle barrel and tell his pa his woes. His pa always told him to hang in there, because a nice lady was on her way. Neither of them believed it, but it made both of them feel better to hear it said.

Well, the day after their latest talk, an old woman who poled her barge through the swamp to deliver milk and eggs to the grocery store had a long talk with Bobby's pa. It seemed she had this daughter who was hankering after a husband with a good steady job, and the old woman thought Bobby would do the job nicely. She suggested they introduce the pair at the next dance, and Bobby's pa agreed.

The night of the dance, Bobby's pa insisted that his son dress in his best. Bobby was dragging his feet a little, remembering all those women who played him false and not wanting to go, but his pa insisted. Well, the moment Bobby clapped eyes on the dark-eyed, red-lipped girl from the swamp, he was head over heels in love. Her eyes sparkled like the sunlight on the bay. Her skin was as creamy as new milk. Her voice was low and sweet.

The pair cuddled and cooed and waltzed the whole night long. Come sunrise Bobby was all for bringing his new love before the visiting priest who delivered his sermons in the grocery store (since there weren't no church in that vicinity) and getting married right away. Well, the girl was willing to get married, but not by a priest.

"Let's just go to the city and have the judge marry us," she said to Bobby, and he was so smitten that he agreed, though it would have been quicker and easier to walk a mile down the road to see the priest.

By the next evening they were wed, and Bobby brought his pretty bride to the little cottage he rented just down the road from the family grocery. It had a nice front porch with a swing, a big bedroom on the second floor, and a big attic with a window that could be made up into a second guestroom should his new mother-in-law care to visit from her home in the swamp.

After fixing him a nice dinner, Bobby's new bride sat awhile in the rocking chair near their bed while Bobby yawned and watched her fondly. She cuddled under the blanket and knitted and hummed while Bobby's eyes grew real heavy and he nodded off. He didn't wake up until early morning, when his new bride crept into bed all hot and sweaty and fell asleep at once. When he asked her where she'd been, she wouldn't answer him. Bobby was mighty sore that his bride had snuck out on him on their wedding night, but she got snappish, and her eyes blazed when he questioned her, so he backed down.

Life took on an odd pattern for Bobby. During the day everything was perfect. His wife was sweet and pretty and loving. She kept the house sparkling clean and cooked him wonderful meals. But each night she refused to come to bed after supper. Like their wedding night, she sat up singing and rocking and knitting until he was asleep, and she did not come to bed till just before dawn. She was always sweaty and cranky when she came to bed, and she went to sleep before Bobby could question her.

Bobby was very confused and upset by this behavior and finally confided in his pa one morning after opening up the grocery store. Bobby's pa was awful worried. The visiting priest had gone on to his next parish, and there was no one else they could consult about the matter except the local conjure woman. So Bobby's pa sent him to her with a couple of chickens as a gift.

The conjure woman knew all about hoodoo magic and was an excellent herbalist. Local folks went to her when they were sick, on account of the doctor lived nigh on twenty miles away. When she heard Bobby's story, she told him to pretend to go to sleep that night and watch what his new bride did. Then he was to come back and tell her everything. Bobby agreed.

The next evening, he pretended to fall asleep while his bride rocked and sang in her chair. Then he followed her up to the attic and watched through the crack in the open door as she sat down at the spinning wheel and spun off her skin, leaving only pulsing red muscles and blue veins. She was a terrifying sight as she sprang through the window and flew away into the night.

Bobby ran out to the privy and was sick after he saw her. Who—what—was this monster he had married? He was still trembling with shock when his bride, looking like a normal person again, crept into bed at dawn, and he had trouble behaving normally at breakfast.

As soon as he could get away, Bobby ran to the home of the conjure woman and told her about the spinning wheel and the terrible skinless creature who flew away from his attic. "A boo-hag," the conjure woman said at once. "You've married a boo-hag."

"What's a boo-hag?" asked Bobby.

"A boo-hag is a witch and a shape-shifter," said the conjure woman. "She lures men into her trap and then delivers them to her boo-daddy, who eats their flesh and gnaws their bones. And that's what she'll do to you if you don't get rid of her first."

Then the conjure woman told Bobby exactly what he needed to do to get rid of the boo-hag. There were two facts, she said, about boo-hags that—when known—could rescue a man from her trap. The first fact was that a boo-hag couldn't fly through a window or door that was painted blue. The second fact was that if a boo-hag didn't get back into her skin before dawn, she would be trapped without it and never again able to disguise herself as a human. So if Bobby got himself some blue paint and spread it on every window frame and every door frame, then the boo-hag could not enter his house and come dawn would be revealed for the monstrous creature she was. However, if Bobby wanted to be rid of the creature entirely, then he should leave one tiny window unpainted and keep it open a sliver so the boo-hag could squeeze through. Then he was to fill up her skin with salt and pepper, which would burn her up from the inside out. By the time she found the unpainted window, the boo-hag would be forced to hurry into her skin or forfeit her human disguise. She wouldn't have time to notice the trap he'd set for her until it was too late!

Bobby promised to do exactly as the conjure woman said. That night, Bobby lingered over his dinner, looking with sad eyes at the pretty woman sitting opposite him. He knew she was really a monster inside, but it was so nice to have a little wife in his home. He hated like anything to see her go. But he didn't want to get eaten by a boo-daddy, and that was his fate if she stayed. So he went up to their bedroom and pretended to fall asleep while she rocked and sang and knitted. Then he followed her quietly upstairs and put salt and pepper into her skin after her ugly, red-muscled, blue-veined figure had flown out the window to her boo-daddy. He spent the rest of the night painting over every door and window frame with blue paint, leaving only one small unpainted window open in the cellar. He nailed it up so that it would open no further than a crack, just as the conjure woman instructed him. Then he hid himself behind a large chest of drawers up in the attic to wait for the boo-hag.

Just before dawn the boo-hag flew up to the attic window. As soon as she touched the blue frame, she gave a shriek of pain and rage. Bobby listened as she flew around the house, testing each window and door and howling like a banshee when it burned her skinless hands. Then she found the little window in the cellar, and he heard the thump as she landed beside it, followed by a painful whimpering sound as she squeezed and squeezed herself through the narrow opening, her skinless red muscles and blue veins tearing painfully against the rough wood.

BOO-HAG

The boo-hag ran up three flights of stairs into the attic and squeezed and squeezed into her skin as fast as she could. She barely got it on when the first light of dawn shone over the horizon. And that was when the salt and pepper did their work, burning the boo-hag's body from the inside out. With a scream of agony, she flung herself out the attic window. Glass shattered everywhere as she tried to fly away, tearing at her skin to get it off. But it was too late. She exploded into tiny pieces right over the swamp, and the fish had a mighty feast of cooked boo-hag for breakfast that morning.

So Bobby was once again without a wife. But bachelorhood looked much better to him after his brief marriage, and he never went looking for a woman again. 'Course, after he made a pile of money in gold and minerals, the girls started chasing him. But that's another story.

14

The Honeymoon

THE SMOKY MOUNTAINS

Mary was thrilled to pieces when George Bolton came a-courting. He was jest about the handsomest man in the mountains—bold, daring, fierce. He was also a good hunter and a good farmer who would be able to provide for a family. And it was awful cute the way he'd run his hands through his dark curls, turn bright red, and stammer when he talked to her. He spent a lot of time staring at his own feet and mumbling when he first started walking her home from church, and he was red as a beet the first evening he came a-sparking to her parents' house. They'd sat on the porch and drank lemonade as the spicy air of the hot summer evening drowsed around them.

After that, George came around most evenings to talk to Mary or bring her presents: a whistle pig he'd shot in the woods, some wild roses he'd found in a clearing, some pretty stones to put in her rock garden. By the end of summer, Mary's mama claimed she was floatin' instead of walkin', and no one was surprised when George proposed marrying around Christmastime. It was the only way they'd get any sense out of Mary, her papa claimed, tapping his girl on the chin. Mary jest grinned at him and kept a tight hold of George's hand.

George spent most of the autumn season constructing a new cabin for his Mary. He found a place in a shady holler on the mountain that was protected from the mountain wind by a tall stand of trees. The holler had a cool, bubbling spring at its center that they could use for water. It was a perfect place for a cabin. The view from the front door, looking out over the valley through a gap in the trees, would be magnificent. And there was a huge flat rock on the ground he could use for both hearthstone and floor. It was pocked with small holes, but his Mary wouldn't mind those, and it made the cabin seem rather posh to have a stone floor.

George finished the cabin around Thanksgiving and carefully shut it up to await the coming of his bride. George and Mary were married at the church the day after Christmas, to a great whooping and hollering and carrying on by their many siblings and cousins and friends. George's brothers threatened to serenade the newlyweds in the middle of the night, and George threatened to knock their blocks off if they did. Though that wouldn't discourage them in the least, Mary remarked as George helped her up into the rough farm wagon he'd borrowed from a neighbor for this ceremonious occasion.

George drove Mary up to the cabin in the light of the swiftly setting sun and showed her around her new home. The one-room cabin had a big loft overhead; there were beehives out back that were going to make their fortune in honey sales; a newly dug privy stood back by the trees; and of course the bubbling spring was only a few feet from the front door. Mary oohed and aahed over every detail, and they sat on the door stoop, snuggling together and admiring the view until the sun set behind the mountains and it grew too dark to see.

Then George carried his bride over the threshold, gave her a gosh-almighty big kiss on the lips that made her giggle and blush happily, and went to build a roaring fire in their new grate. After cooking some dinner, the happy honeymooners retired to bed and cuddled together under the thick eiderdown.

"Yer brothers are gonna come serenading us sometime tonight," Mary told her new husband sleepily.

"Yep. No doubt," George mumbled, already nodding off in the warmth of the fire.

Mary smiled and curled herself a little closer to her new husband. In a few moments they were both asleep.

They were both awakened abruptly out of a deep sleep by a slimy, slithery, hissing sort of sound that was getting louder by the minute. "Is that yer brothers?" Mary asked, rolling over and rubbing her eyes. "I expected them to play the banjo at least!"

"I ain't sure what it is," George said. "I'll build up the fire, and we can check."

George slipped out of bed, his feet hitting the pocked stone floor, which was still warm from the blaze they'd made earlier. He walked toward the glowing coals in the fireplace, one step, two. And his foot landed on something squirmy and round and scaly. A snake! It hissed and rattled at him, and he became aware suddenly that the dark floor was alive with hissing rattlesnakes. They writhed all around his feet and legs, and he felt the horrible sting as their fangs struck his bare legs over and over.

"Rattlers!" George gasped desperately to his bride. "They must have been sleeping under the stone and come up through the holes when they sensed the heat of the fire! Get under that ciderdown right now, Mary! Right now! Cover yerself up and *don't move!*"

George could feel poison filling up his body. He staggered another step—he didn't really know where he wanted to go anymore or why. The snakes were climbing his body . . . or perhaps he had fallen down among them. His body was ablaze with pain, and he felt so tired. So tired . . .

Mary, sobbing softly in horror and fear, slid underneath the thick eiderdown and lay very, very still. She heard George moving for a few moments more. Then there was silence save for the slithering, rattling, and hissing of the snakes. Several times during that endless night, she felt snakes sliding back and forth over the eiderdown, and one large snake seemed to have taken up residence across her feet. She didn't dare move.

Just before dawn, there came the crashing sound of saucepans being banged together right outside the window. Mary jumped at the sound, but the snakes didn't notice the tiny movement she made under the eiderdown. They had stopped moving around so much once the temperature inside the cabin had cooled down. The tinny sound of a bugle being played poorly accompanied the slamming saucepans, and then somebody kicked in with a banjo. Mary could hear her brothers-in-law singing a bawdy song. Somebody knocked on the front door and then banged it open. She heard her brothers-in-law march over the doorsill with their heavy boots and then heard them gasp in horror, the song abruptly grinding to a halt as all three of them saw the bloated body of their brother George lying on the floor, surrounded by rattlers grown sluggish in the chilly morning air.

One of the men, seeing the lump on the bed, called: "Hang on, Mary! We're coming." Then the men set to work, grimly killing snake after snake and tossing the bodies in the

THE HONEYMOON

corner. When it was safe, they pulled Mary out from under the eiderdown, surprised and relieved to find her alive. But the ordeal had turned her lovely golden curls snow white, and her face was ever afterward lined with wrinkles like those of a woman twice her age. The cabin was closed up forever, and Mary went back home to live with her folks.

These days, if anyone chances to walk near that old holler at night, they will often hear sounds coming from the derelict cabin with the pocked stone floor. Despairing shouts, the hiss and rattle of snakes, and clear as day, a man's voice shouting: "Don't move, Mary. *Don't move!*"

15

The Carpenter

BAT CAVE

J. J. Tucker owned a big farm just south of Bat Cave, and he was just about as prosperous as a man could be. All his horses and cows were plump and fit, his barns were watertight and filled with hay and grain for the winter, and his wife was pleasant and downright pretty to boot. J. J.'s only sorrow was for his little boy Arnie, who'd had a crippled leg ever since he fell off the wagon and got run over by a wheel.

J. J. Tucker had a generous heart toward most every person he met. If any passing peddler stopped at his gate, he'd purchase some of his wares, whether needed or not. Anyone down on their luck would soon find a dollar in their pockets, courtesy of J. J. Tucker, and could sit down to a good meal made by his missus anytime they felt a little hungry. He gave generously to the church and was right up on the roof with the other men helping with repairs after a big storm.

Considering his big heart and generous spirit, folks considered it strange that J. J. and his next-door neighbor—once the best of friends—were no longer on speaking terms. But Ted Franklin and J. J. Tucker had argued strenuously over the ownership of the property that lay between their farms, and in the end they'd stopped speaking to each other. Worse, Ted Franklin dug a deep ditch between the two properties and diverted a small stream into it to further separate the once-friendly neighbors, one from the other.

Not long after the ditch was dug, a stranger came strolling up the lane toward J. J. Tucker's farm. J. J., just done with the morning milking, came to the gate to meet him, all smiles. J. J. greeted the man gladly, and the stranger said, "I'm a carpenter looking for a day's work. Someone told me you might have a job for me."

J. J. beamed with delight. "I do indeed," he said, opening the farm gate wide and inviting the carpenter through.

J. J. led the carpenter to the footpath that once joined his farm with his neighbor's. "See that stream over there," he said to the carpenter. "My neighbor Ted dug that stream after we had a falling-out over some land. Now I aim to do him one better. I'd like you to build a big fence right along the edge of that ditch so he can't see my farm anymore. There's poles and fencing in the barn just here. Think you can do it?"

The carpenter studied the situation for a moment. "I think I can build something you'd like," he said at last.

"Capital!" said J. J. Tucker. "I'll nip to the upper field after breakfast to chop some weed. Meantime, come break bread with us!" The carpenter smiled and accepted the breakfast invitation.

Little Arnie was quite taken with the carpenter when J. J. brought him to the house. The little boy talked and talked excitedly during the meal, and he watched from the window when the man headed down the footpath with his toolbox.

"Mama, can I watch the carpenter work?" he pleaded, limping around to face his plump mother, who was busy kneading bread at the large kitchen table.

"If he says you can," said his fond mother. "But don't talk his ear off like you did at breakfast."

Little Arnie grinned and promised his mother before maneuvering slowly out the door with his crutch. Dragging his twisted leg behind him, he limped slowly down the footpath, the crutch thumping in the dirt. He stopped a few feet from where the carpenter was working and asked if he could watch for a while. The man looked up with a smile so sweet and tender that Little Arnie's heart swelled with joy. "Of course you may," the carpenter said, and Little Arnie sat down on a stump to watch the man sawing boards to the proper length and then nailing them to the frame.

All day long the carpenter worked as Little Arnie sat and watched. The carpenter had a splendid voice and sang many songs for the delighted child. He was also a storyteller and told Arnie wonderful tales about faraway places and interesting people.

At noon, Missus Tucker brought them a basket of fried chicken to eat, and they supped together, the best of pals. The day sped by on wings. Little Arnie could not remember when he had enjoyed himself so much.

The carpenter finished his work just before supper. He cleaned up the job site and then walked back to the house easy and slow, so the little boy could keep up without hurting his twisted leg. So kindly was this done that Little Arnie never realized that the carpenter had slowed his customary pace to accommodate him.

THE CARPENTER

As they reached the house, J. J. Tucker bustled out with a huge smile. "Done then?" he asked jovially.

"Done, indeed. Come see," said the carpenter.

As the men turned back toward the footpath, the carpenter stopped a moment and laid his hand on Little Arnie's head. He smiled down at the child. "Go in to your mother now, and leave your crutch by the door when you go in," he said. "Thank you for the company today."

"You're welcome," the little boy said happily, turning toward the door.

The carpenter and J. J. walked down the footpath together, and a moment later, J. J. stopped dead in the center of the trail. A beautifully sculpted bridge spanned the stream in the place where he had asked the carpenter to construct a fence. And crossing the bridge, hand outstretched in delighted greeting, was Ted Franklin! Before J. J. could process what had happened, indeed, before he could even exclaim in surprise, his neighbor had seized his right hand and was pumping it up and down.

"Bless you, J. J. Bless you ten times over," Ted cried. "I was miserable after I dug that ditch. I wanted us to be friends again, but somehow I could never bring myself to say so. Now you've built this bridge to join our land together again, and I can't thank you enough!"

Finally regaining his voice, J. J. said, "I've wanted to be friends too. But I was too proud to say so. Much as I'd like to claim credit for the bridge, it was the carpenter here who built the bridge."

The neighbors both turned and beamed upon the carpenter, who heaved his toolbox up onto his shoulder and nodded at them. Then he vanished.

The men gasped and reeled back on their heels in astonishment. Where had the carpenter gone?

At that very moment, there came a shout of "Daddy" from the direction of the house. The neighbors turned and looked toward the house, just as Little Arnie came pelting down the footpath. He was running as fast as ever a boy could run; his twisted leg had been made whole again the instant he had laid his crutch by the door.

Little Arnie threw himself into his father's arms. Tears rolling down his cheeks, J. J. swept his son up and shouted: "Praise be! Oh, praise be!"

The two neighbors exchanged a look over Little Arnie's head and then glanced as one toward the bridge.

"He healed a child and built a bridge," Ted murmured thoughtfully. "I wonder . . ."

Hugging his little boy tight, J. J. smiled at his neighbor and said, "Perhaps we should just say: Thank God for the carpenter."

"Amen," Ted said heartily. "Amen."

16

Doppelgänger

By the time the doctor left the house, it was only an hour or so before dawn. He was weary almost beyond bearing, for the birth had taken nearly twenty-four hours, but the good master of the house and his lady now had a healthy pair of twins who were bawling mightily for food when the doctor departed.

"Come, Gray. Let's go home," the doctor sighed, saddling up his patient gray horse. Gray turned calm eyes on his old friend and nuzzled the doctor's face, knocking his hat awry. The doctor smiled and patted the horse on the nose.

Swinging wearily into the saddle, the doctor rode out of the farmyard and into the dark lane. "I'm getting too old for this kind of life, Gray," the doctor said to his horse as they clip-clopped down the farm lane toward the main road. The horse snorted as if in answer to the doctor's words. The doctor laughed and said, "It's true. My father dropped dead when he was sixty-two, and I turned sixty-two last week." The doctor sighed heavily and was silent for a few moments as they turned onto the main road, heading toward Boone.

"They say," the doctor continued aloud after a few minutes of plodding, "that Father saw his doppelgänger a few days before he passed. Do you know what a doppelgänger is, Gray?" He reached forward and patted his horse on the neck. Gray tossed his head a bit, perking his ears back to show his old friend that he was listening.

"I wasn't sure myself, so I looked it up when I heard the story from Mother. A doppelgänger is a ghostly double of yourself. To see yourself repeated thus is an omen of death." The doctor shook his head, white hair slipping out from under the hat to flop across his forehead. Weary to his bones, he fell silent again. It was hard work to sit upright against the gentle swaying of Gray's back.

The woods around them were filled with the soft rustles of foxes and other night creatures searching for food. The crickets sang softly, and once an owl hooted right overhead, startling the doctor and Gray. Occasionally, the doctor would catch a glimpse of the starry sky between the leaves overhead, and here and there shafts of pure-white moonlight pierced the dark canopy and created lovely beams that illuminated the road ahead.

"Mother told me that Father walked out on the front porch one morning and saw himself walking up the front path," the doctor said to Gray as they entered a beam of moonlight. For a moment doctor and horse glowed white, as if they had turned into ghostly doubles. "The doppelgänger went right past Father and through the front door, but when Father followed it inside, it was gone." They stepped out of the moonbeam into the shadows and entered the Big Laurel—a section of the woods that was densely tangled with laurel ivy and other mountain timber. It was said to be haunted by the spirit of a headless dog, but the doctor and Gray had never seen it, and they rode this way nearly every day.

Ahead of them, the road made a hairpin turn around a giant fallen tree. There was a break in the canopy of laurel and timber where the giant tree had once been. The moonlight shone down through the break, illuminating the road on either side of the fallen tree. As the doctor drew closer to the moonbeam on this section of road, he realized—between one blink and the next—that a dark figure on horseback was approaching the moonbeam on the far side of the tree.

In the distance the church bell tolled out five times for 5:00 a.m. as the doctor and Gray stepped into the moonbeam together. The doctor glanced across the fallen tree and found himself staring at a man wearing a dark coat and hat, with a strand of white hair slipping down on his forehead. The man's face was a mirror of the doctor's, and his horse was a mirror of Gray.

The doctor's mouth dropped open. His heart stuttered and then began to thunder against his ribs in shock. Gray didn't appear to notice the ghostly visitation. He kept moving forward out of the moonbeam. As soon as they entered the shadowy bend that led to the far side of the log, the vision vanished. Then they rounded the hairpin bend, and the doctor could see the trembling moonbeam where the horseman had stood but a moment before. The moonbeam was empty. A moment later, Gray plowed right through it and kept going.

The doctor slumped forward, heart pounding and legs trembling visibly against the sides of his horse. Confused, Gray stopped, turning his ears back and forth, trying to understand what his old friend wanted him to do. The doctor drew in one ragged breath, then another. Slowly he sat up. "Walk on, Gray," he told his faithful steed, and the horse stepped forward obediently.

DOPPELGÄNGER

The doctor's heart rate was so high now that he felt dizzy and sick. As Gray approached the next farm lane, the doctor turned his old horse into it and went up to the house. The night was shifting into the gray dimness of early morning, and the doctor knew the farmer would be getting up to milk his cows. In fact, the farmer was just leaving through the side door of the house when the doctor fell off his horse at the gate. The farmer—an old acquaintance of the doctor's—hurried over to help him into the house. The good lady of the house thrust him into a chair, gave him a hot cup of tea dosed with whiskey, and cut him some bread and cheese to eat.

The whole family soon gathered around, and the doctor told everyone about the figure he'd seen in the Big Laurel at the bend in the road. He told them that the phantom rode a gray horse, but he could not bring himself to mention that he'd seen his own face on the horseman. Some things were meant to be private. Besides, he might be mistaken. He'd been thinking about doppelgängers and death omens all evening, and he was very tired from the birthing.

The farmer, seeing the doctor's weariness, had his eldest son drive the doctor home with old Gray tied behind the wagon. The doctor entered his front door shortly after dawn, pausing just long enough to give a weary wave to the cheerful boy who was leading Gray to the stable for him. His worried wife met him in the front hall and led him upstairs. As they mounted the steps, the doctor told his wife all about the vision he'd seen at the Big Laurel. He finished the tale as he stepped over the threshold of his bedroom. His weary eyes were on the warm comfort of the large bed he shared with his spouse when he felt a shooting pain in his arm that rose up and up until it encompassed his whole body in one bright flash. The doctor fell heavily to the floor and did not hear his wife's scream.

For two days, the doctor lay in a coma after his massive heart attack. He died just before dawn on the third day, just as the church bell tolled out five times for 5:00 a.m.

Dreams and Visions

PINEOLA

Aunt Sally looked up from her spinning wheel with a smile when she heard the knock on her door. Aunt Sally loved company, and she'd been feeling a tad lonely that afternoon, what with everyone out in the fields working the harvest. She brushed off her apron, tidied her hair, and went to open the door. Standing there, hat in hand, was her nephew Blake.

"Well, Blake! Come on in," Aunt Sally cried happily. She pulled her nephew in the door, set him down at the table, and got him a drink of cider.

Blake smiled at his aunt over the rim of his cup and said, "My Betty's a mite nervous at spending the night alone in our cabin. She was wondering if you'd come stay with her while I'm away doing the rounds." Blake sold tinware for a living, and often he'd take to the road for five to ten days at a time to peddle his wares.

"I'd be happy to," Aunt Sally said, beaming with delight. "Let me pack up a few things, and we can go right now!"

Blake gave a sigh of relief. He didn't know what he'd do if Aunt Sally had said no. It wasn't just that Betty would fret. He was also worried about their neighbor Ralph, who had once sparked with Betty before she met Blake. Ralph was still interested in Blake's pretty wife, of that he was certain. What Blake didn't know was how his wife felt about her old beau. It worried him, because he was on the road a lot, and Betty got lonesome. Having Aunt Sally around would keep a lid on things, Blake was sure.

Betty greeted Aunt Sally with relief, and the two ladies were happily planning out their time together when Blake left on his rounds. They would work on Betty's new quilt, and Aunt Sally would spin while Betty knitted and would help harvest the honey from the beehives out back. And there were apples to pick and canning to do. The time would just speed past.

A few days into this promising agenda, Betty came down with a nasty cough, and Aunt Sally put her to bed with a mustard plaster. Then she settled down in a comfortable chair with her knitting and drowsed the evening away, rousing herself occasionally to put a log on the fire. Finally, she laughed to herself, wondering why she was bothering to stay up.

Aunt Sally went over to the bed where Betty lay sleeping and pulled the trundle bed from underneath it. But before she could step into it, the front door blew open with a crash, and a tall man, dark featured, with a horned head, hooves instead of feet, and a lashing tail stepped into the room and pointed a finger at Sally. Behind him, Sally could just see writhing, dancing figures—women, children, and black hellcats—against a backdrop of red flames.

"Beware," the devil-man called. "Beware!" Then the devil, the flames, and the dancers all vanished as suddenly as they arrived, and Sally found herself still kneeling next to the trundle bed in the flickering firelight, ready to crawl inside. Shaking from head to toe, Aunt Sally dove under the covers and prayed for the Lord to spare her and Betty from evil. Finally, she fell into a disturbed sleep and woke unrefreshed in the morning.

Betty's cold had really taken hold by then, so Aunt Sally spent most of the day nursing her niece by marriage and working at the spinning wheel. When Betty fell asleep in the afternoon, Aunt Sally slipped outside to gather pine knots. She wanted a big bright fire in the hearth tonight in case that devil-man came back. The cabin was awful dark at night, and the pine knots would help illuminate the dark cabin and keep the devil from the door. At least Aunt Sally hoped they would. She put a great big pile of pine knots by the chimney and then went to tend Betty, who was stirring restlessly against the pillows.

Aunt Sally kept the fire blazing with pine knots all evening while Betty slept. Finally, she decided that the devil-man wasn't coming back. Sighing with relief, she crept over to the bed and pulled out the trundle. Immediately, the front door slammed open and the darkly wicked devil-man stepped inside, eyes blazing red like the flames silhouetting him. Aunt Sally could see the dancers again. She counted nine women, four children, and nine black hellcats.

As the devil advanced into the room, one of the black hellcats scrambled through the door and sprang into the fire, rolling happily about and batting at the pine knots. "Here, you. Get out of there," Aunt Sally scolded, forgetting the devil-man for a moment. She dearly loved cats—even black ones—and didn't want it to get burned. She strode over to the fire and glared down at the black cat. It yawned, rolled over on its back, and stared lazily up at her with amber eyes.

Aunt Sally sensed movement behind her. She whirled away from the fire and glared at the devil-man, who was standing over the bed with a vial of blood in his hand, dripping the blood down onto Betty's pretty white fingers.

"You! Stop that right now," Aunt Sally said, angry now. "Get out of here! Both of you. Right now." Seizing a blazing branch from the fire, she swatted at the black cat and then used it like a sword, feinting left and right at the devil. He laughed, pocketed the vial of blood, and calmly caught the blazing end of the branch in his hands. Then he bowed to Aunt Sally and vanished.

Once again, Aunt Sally found herself kneeling next to the trundle bed in the flickering firelight, ready to crawl inside. "Lord have mercy! It must be a vision of some kind," she muttered. "But I don't want to know what kind of vision has the devil in it!"

Grimly, Aunt Sally crawled into the trundle bed and said her prayers, begging the Lord to spare her and Betty from evil. But somehow she wasn't comforted by her prayers. She fell into a restless sleep and dreamed . . .

She dreamed of a dark night with no moon or stars. The fireplace was filled to the top with pine knots, but the light did not reach more than a foot beyond the hearth. And just outside the door came the sound of digging.

Aunt Sally rose slowly from the trundle bed and dragged one weary foot after another to the front door. She did not want to see what was outside, but something morbid and dark compelled her forward. She opened the door and stared outside at a group of men digging a grave, surrounded—oddly enough—by a flock of chickens. They had to keep shooing the chickens out of the

DREAMS AND VISIONS

open grave. To the right of the grave diggers, Aunt Sally saw a hand thrust forth out of the apple tree holding a white-handled knife. The knife began pruning away the small twigs from the tree, which tumbled to the ground beneath it.

Then Aunt Sally heard a grunting sound and the thud of hooves. Turning, she saw a big white ox with black spots walking up the trail toward the cabin. A man was riding the ox, but she couldn't see his face. Wondering what the knife wielder would do when it—he?—saw the ox rider, she turned to look at the apple tree. But the hand with the knife was gone, leaving only a number of pruned twigs on the ground. Bewildered, Aunt Sally turned again to the ox rider and saw the man lying flat on the ground, and the ox settling itself down on the ground next to the man, waiting patiently for its master to rise.

Then everything vanished and the world went dark . . .

And Aunt Sally awoke to the cheerful jingling of a wagonload of tinware coming up the trail toward the house. She'd overslept! Blake was almost home, and there was no breakfast on the table to greet him. Forgetting all about her dream, she woke Betty, who was feeling much better by now, and scurried about getting breakfast for her nephew.

It was only when Aunt Sally was back in her cozy cottage on her son's property that she remembered her visions and the dream that had followed them. Blood dripping on Betty's white fingers, the open grave, the white-handled knife, the spotted ox, and the devil-man saying, "Beware!"

About a week after she returned home, Aunt Sally opened the front door to let in some fresh air, and a small black cat walked inside. It trotted over to the fireplace, batted at one of the logs in the grate, and then turned big amber eyes up at

Aunt Sally and said, "Mere." It was the spittin' image of the cat in Aunt Sally's vision. Alarmed, she said, "Is something wrong with Betty, cat?"

The black cat blinked once and pawed a loose pine knot sitting in the log basket.

Taking that as a yes, Aunt Sally grabbed her shawl and headed out to her son Sam's place. She'd ask Sam to drive her to Blake and Betty's cabin back in the woods. She was climbing the steps to the porch when Blake himself rode up, calling for Sam.

"What's happened?" Aunt Sally cried, staring into her nephew's grim, despairing face as Sam barreled out onto the porch, alarmed by Blake's frantic call.

"Betty's run off with that old spark of hers—Ralph," Blake said grimly. "Her brother Bill's gone after them with his gun. He's furious. I think he may kill Ralph *and* Betty if he meets up with them."

Sam ran for his horse. Aunt Sally watched as the two cousins rode off into the hills to locate the fleeing lovers before the murderous Bill. Somehow, in her heart, she knew it was already too late. She went home and fed the little black cat that— mercifully—lay on a blanket *beside* the hearth, unlike the cat in her vision.

It was Sam who came, many hours later, and sat beside his mother's hearth with the black cat in his lap to tell her the last part of the story. Ralph and Betty had taken to the wild mountain paths in their bid for freedom. They took turns riding Ralph's big white ox with the black spots, switching places every time the person on foot grew weary.

Unbeknownst to the lovers, Betty's brother Bill discovered their trail and climbed the hill in front of them. Finding a fallen apple tree, he pruned away the twigs using his white-handled knife to make a perfect blind for his rifle. When Ralph and Betty came up the hill—Ralph riding the black-spotted ox— Bill shot Ralph dead. Betty fled back the way they'd come, and Bill followed her, leaving his white-handled knife by the fallen apple tree. When Blake and Sam arrived, they found Ralph lying dead on the path with his big black-spotted ox lying patiently beside him, waiting for his owner to get up. It was Blake who'd found Bill's white-handled knife and pieced together what had happened. By this time Bill had fled from the mountains— fearing retribution from the authorities—after giving his sister the scolding of her life.

Aunt Sally dabbed at her eyes with her handkerchief, remembering the blood the devil-man had dripped on Betty's hands in her vision. It must have been Ralph's blood, and her niece-in-law would have it on her conscience for the rest of her days.

They buried Ralph on top of the hill. While they were digging the grave, a free-roaming flock of chickens kept pecking around the path and flying into the open grave, much to the annoyance of the grave diggers. So Aunt Sally's dream was fulfilled in every particular.

Betty never strayed from her marriage vows again. And Aunt Sally still has a little black cat with amber eyes that always seems to know exactly what she is thinking. But the devil-man never returned, for which all were thankful.

The Coffin

FAYETTEVILLE

Bang! Bang! Bang!

The sharp sound roused me from sleep at 3:00 a.m., according to the chiming of the grandfather clock in the hall. I sat up, startled by the noise.

Bang! Bang! Bang!

I heard the sound again. This time my befuddled head made sense of the noise. It was the sound of someone banging a nail with a hammer. And it was coming from the shop next door. From *my* carpenter shop, in fact!

I shook my wife, Lizzie, awake and said, "Honey! Somebody's in the shop. I'm going to see who it is, and *howdy boy*, are they going to be in trouble when I get through with them!"

Lizzie sat up sleepily.

"It's probably some fool kids messing about," she said as I struggled into my britches. "I'd better check on the baby. If them fool kids woke her up after it took me three ages to get her to sleep, they're gonna feel the edge of my tongue!"

From the workshop next door came the thump of heavy wood being moved about, and then a very loud sawing noise. Tossing my nightcap on the bed, I struggled into my shirt and ran

THE COFFIN

downstairs to get my rifle while Lizzie checked on our two-year-old daughter. I filled it with rock salt, which stings like the dickens and gets the point across without actually hurting anybody. Then I was out the front door and running toward my shop.

First thing I noticed: It was dark in there. Way too dark for someone to be messing about with hammer and saw unless they was aiming to injure themselves. I slowed down to a trot, wondering what was going on. For a moment, the shop was silent. Then the bang-bang-banging of the hammer started again. I could hear it clearly coming from the carpenter shop, though there was nothing to see. I squinted at the shop, puzzled and a bit frightened. Then I perceived a faint blue glow and smiled grimly to myself. Aha! I headed for the door, my gun ready to "persuade" any kids messing around inside to leave be and go home.

I yanked the door open. There was no one inside. At least no one visible. Instead, I saw a glowing blue coffin laid out on sawhorses in the center of the shop. A hammer hovered over it. As I watched, it started banging another nail into place. Then the saw rose up and started cutting another board to the proper size to fit the side of the coffin.

I gasped, my heart banging even harder than the hammer. Cold chills ran up the outside of my arms, and all my muscles froze. What was this uncanny thing? My stomach started flip-flopping inside my gut, and the hairs on my scalp prickled. In that moment little details sprang out at me. The coffin was made of cedar. It cast no shadow on the floor. The hammer was a new one I had never seen before. I could see the outline of my saw resting on the bench, and yet somehow it was also hovering in the air, teeth sawing into the phantom board.

Suddenly, the light went out, and the coffin vanished along with the floating hammer and saw. My heart gave a painful stutter, and my legs unfroze. With a terrified shriek, I staggered backward out the door, clutching my rifle.

"Haints! We're being hainted!" I raced back to the house, put my gun on the rack over the door, and ran upstairs to the bedroom to tell Lizzie what I'd seen in the shop. Lizzie's eyes got real big as she listened, and she clutched the quilt up to her chin as I told her about the glowing coffin.

"That ain't haints, Jed," she said to me. "That there's a premonition, that's what it is. Somebody's gonna die, and your gonna build them a cedar coffin for the buryin'. I'm sure of it."

I hadn't thought of that. I sank down on the edge of the bed. "My great-granny up in Nova Scotia calls them forerunners," I said thoughtfully. "Lights and sounds and visions ya see jest before a person passes. I dint think we got 'em here in the Carolinas."

"People get 'em everywhere," said Lizzie. "There ain't nothing you can do 'bout that premonition now, Jed, so come to bed."

She was right, of course. I sighed and slipped under the covers. But it took me a long time to go to sleep.

I weren't too surprised the next morning when we got word that Lizzie's aunt had passed in the night. It was 3:00 a.m. when she died, the same hour we'd heard the ghostly noises in the carpenter shop. Lizzie's uncle James stopped by the house to give us the sad news, and he asked me to build a coffin for his wife out of cedar, her favorite tree. To thank me for my trouble, he went out and bought me a brand-new hammer for the shop.

It was the same one I'd seen floating in the air over the glowing coffin. I nearly dropped it when he first handed it to me.

It felt plumb awkward setting out the sawhorses and cutting up the boards that day. I kept remembering how I'd sort of seen myself doing it last night, and the thought made my hands shake. But someone had to make a coffin out of respect for Lizzie's aunt that passed.

I made the prettiest cedar coffin I could with all sorts of fancy scrollwork, and I polished it up good so you could see your face in the wood. Uncle James was s'pleased with that coffin. It did his wife proud, he said. But I could hardly bear to look at it. It didn't feel right to me, as if seeing the glowing coffin in my shop had somehow made me responsible fer the death of Lizzie's aunt. Which my wife said was nonsense.

Maybe so. But I never went out to investigate any more mysterious noises coming from my shop. I'd had enough of premonitions to last me a lifetime.

Resurrection

CHARLOTTE

I suppose, looking back, that we could have found a less grisly way to make some money. But at the time jobs were scarce, and a university fellow needed to have some spare change if he wanted to make an impression on the pretty local girls. At least that's what we thought.

It was Charlie who first suggested that we might assist the local medical school in their search for cadavers. He was studying to be a doctor and had heard rumors of the ghost of a girl that supposedly haunted his college. Folks said her body had been stolen and brought to the school for medical research, and her ghost had haunted the school ever since. That's what gave him the idea.

Charlie found out from the friend of a friend that there was money to be had for fresh corpses on the black market. That's when he roped in me and Lester. Three of us could haul around corpses better than just one. Lester and I were a bit dubious at first about Charlie's proposition. I'd been all set to interview for a job at the local pharmacy, and Lester was about to apply for work at the newspaper. But Charlie was persuasive. We could earn more in one night grave robbing than we could earn in a month of honest toil at the pharmacy or the newspaper. Besides, once a person has passed, he or she didn't need the body anymore. Said so right in the Good Book. They were getting a new one, come Judgment Day. *And* we'd be advancing the cause of science. Well, I was in favor of advancing the cause of science. And Lester was always short of money. So we agreed to Charlie's plan.

We chose a moonless night for our first adventure. Lester and Charlie had been scouting all the churches and graveyards in the vicinity, and I'd been watching the newspapers for funeral announcements. Between us, we came up with a couple of good candidates who'd shuffled off the mortal coil in the last few days. As soon as it got dark, we went to work.

"First up, a man named Jonathan Smith," Lester announced as he slid onto the seat of the wagon and picked up the reins.

"Sounds like a pseudonym," said Charlie, sliding in next to him. "I wonder what crime he was hiding."

Soon we were trotting down the road toward a cemetery south of town. We quickly came abreast of a wrought-iron fence that announced the start of the cemetery. Lester cautiously nosed the wagon inside the gates and drove to a corner lot, where the lantern Charlie was holding showed a new headstone and recently disturbed earth. Glancing at the headstone, I read: "Sacred to the memory of my husband Jonathan. His comely young widow yearns to be comforted." Lester laughed when he saw the stone and said, "Here you go, Charlie. You can spark with the Widow Smith!"

I shook my head and handed around the shovels. It was slow, hot work digging up a coffin. We shoveled the dirt onto a canvas tarp laid by the grave, so the nearby grounds remained

RESURRECTION

pristine. We started the digging at the head of the grave clear to the coffin. We covered the lid in sacking to muffle noise, and Lester used a crowbar to pull it free. And there was Mr. Jonathan Smith, resurrected at last, though perhaps not the way he'd been expecting.

The old man was not good to look upon when we pulled him out. Widow Smith had decked him out in his best suit, but his white hair flopped wildly as we lifted him up, and nothing could improve the collapsed, withered look to his face or the greenish tint of his skin in the lantern light. And he smelled awful. Still, money was money. Charlie and I hauled the corpse to the wagon while Lester started filling in the grave. We laid Mr. Smith in back and then helped Lester smooth down the dirt by the headstone. I tossed the canvas on top of Mr. Smith's body to conceal it as we got back into the wagon.

Our second snatch had been buried in a cemetery a little to the east of town. We headed out that way in high spirits. We were going to make a fortune! The only light along the tree-lined avenue came from Charlie's lantern. It made strange flickering shadows on the underside of the branches. You don't realize how noisy the night is— what with the buzz of chirping insects, the rustle of night creatures roaming the bushes, and the calling of night birds—until all that sound ceases abruptly, as it had now. And from somewhere in back of the wagon, a moaning sound began. "*Oooo. Ooooo!*"

The sound started low but grew in volume and rose in pitch until it echoed up and down the shadowy lane and the whole wagon shook with it. My ears hurt, and my teeth buzzed unpleasantly, but that was nothing compared to the shudders of fear shaking my body and the chills crawling all over my skin.

"Cut it out, Charlie. That isn't funny," Lester shouted as the horses nervously swerved first to one side of the road and then to the other, their ears pricked backward in anxiety. His hands were shaking on the reins as we broke out of the tree line into a wide meadow with a cow pond on our left.

"It isn't me!" Charlie retorted over the escalating sound. He clapped shaking hands over his ears and turned to look back over the seat of the wagon. The dirty tarp was shaking as something struggled to rise from underneath. And then a green light came streaming up through the tarp, shooting over our heads like a bright firework, and started spinning in the air. It rapidly formed into the figure of a skinny old man with a withered face and floppy white hair. He flew right at us, fingers outstretched like claws.

Lester shouted in panic. The horses reared and then plunged off the road, racing down the incline and into the shallow pond. The ghost flew after us; his glowing hands pummeled our faces and pulled at our hair. Every blow was ice cold, as if we were being slapped with winter sea water. Behind us, the moaning sound increased until I thought my eardrums would burst. The horses were chest deep in water and trying desperately to swim, but the wagon stuck fast in the muddy bottom and pulled them to a halt.

I leapt out of the wagon into the pond with a great splash. I waded as fast as I could through muddy water and bulrushes, chased by the irate ghost. As soon as I hit dry land, I ran for my life. The glowing man whirled back toward the wagon and pummeled the escaping Charlie and Lester around the ears as they followed me up the slope and down the road. I risked a quick look behind me and saw the moaning corpse of Jonathan

Smith rolling in the wagon bed, all tangled up in the tarp. The glowing ghost swooped and tried to free his corpse from the tarp, but his spirit hands were unable to grip it. The horses rolled their eyes in panic but were stuck fast and unable to flee from the frightening vision. I kept running.

Fatigue forced us to a halt, and we lay panting in the center of the dark avenue. We knew we had to go back. We couldn't leave the wagon and the horses in the pond. "And," I said aloud, "we have to rebury the body."

Charlie groaned but didn't argue with me. None of us wanted to mess with moaning corpses or savage ghosts for the rest of our lives.

We waited until the shrieks of outrage had ceased before we crept back along the avenue and crouched at the edge of the tree line, looking for the ghost. All was silent in the meadow, and the horses were shifting restlessly in the water as they tried in vain to free themselves from the harness. The body in the wagon bed had ceased moaning and lay still.

Hastily, we pushed and pulled at the wagon until it came unstuck from the pond mud, and we guided the trembling horses out of the pond and back up the hill. Then Lester drove at top speed back to the cemetery, and we re-interred Jonathan Smith next to the stone put up by his hopeful widow. It was full daylight before we got to Lester's house, and we still had to wash the mud off the wagon before we called it quits for the night.

"Shall we go again tomorrow?" Charlie asked half-heartedly when the last bit of mud was removed. Lester and I glared at him. "Or maybe not," he mumbled, backing away hastily. "I'll see you both later." He hastened out of the barn and ran out of the yard, a rumpled figure in water-stained trousers and weedy boots.

"There's got to be a better way to earn money," I said to Lester as I tossed a dirty rag into the rain barrel.

"I'm going to work for the newspaper," Lester said flatly. "And I refuse to cover the obits."

He walked out of the barn without looking back. I watched him go ruefully and then headed home myself. If I hurried, I could get cleaned up and still make that job interview at the pharmacy. Even if I didn't get the position, I was sure of one thing: My body-snatching days were over! I'd find some other way of earning cash.

20

The White Deer

There is a legend told of a time long ago when a group of English colonists bravely left their homes to travel to a new world. They settled on the island of Roanoke, and while they were there, a small girl-child was born to the daughter of the new governor. The baby was named Virginia in honor of Elizabeth I, the Virgin Queen.

Concerned for the well-being of his small colony, the governor traveled back to his homeland for supplies—and found himself trapped there by a war between England and Spain. For three years he was kept from his beloved daughter, his new grandchild, and the good people who had settled in his colony. Finally, he boarded a ship and sailed for the New World and for the City of Raleigh he'd left behind.

The governor arrived on Roanoke Island on August 18, 1590—his granddaughter's third birthday—and found it empty. No welcoming daughter and son-in-law. No toddling grandbaby. No settlers. The City of Raleigh was deserted, plundered, and surrounded by a palisade of great trees, as if it were a fort. On one of the palisades, he found the single word *croatoan* carved into the surface, and the letters *cro* carved into a nearby tree.

Hoping this meant that the colony (and his family) had gone to stay with his friend Chief Manteo on present-day Hatteras Island, the governor was preparing to follow them when a great hurricane arose, damaging his ships and forcing him to return to England. He was never able to fund another trip to America and died without knowing what had happened to his family. Indeed, no one ever found out what happened to the Lost Colony. It remains a mystery to this day.

But the whispers of American legend tell a further story about the lost colonists. Not the story of a people slaughtered or a people lost. It is a story of a family displaced from their home by the hostility of island natives, a story of a family taken in by a neighboring tribe on the far side of the island and welcomed with open arms. And it is the story of a little baby girl with bright blue eyes and long flowing hair who was beloved by all who met her and much missed by her grieving grandfather, who died alone in England.

Virginia Dare grew wise in the ways of the forest, strong in her understanding of man and beast. And with each year she grew more comely and desirable until all the eligible warriors in the tribe were in love with her. The young chief Okisko was the bravest and the most handsome of the warriors, and his suit found favor with the lovely Virginia Dare, and with her doting parents. But the medicine man Chico was not pleased by the match. He desired the lovely girl for himself and would not allow her to go to another. A wizard coached in the dark arts, he called on the spirits and caused a spell to fall upon Virginia Dare, transforming her into a white deer as she walked alone near the sound one summer evening. With a bleat of fear and confusion, the white deer fled into the trees and bracken, lost to the sight of the cunning sorcerer.

THE WHITE DEER

The Dare family was alarmed when their daughter did not return from her stroll that evening. Everyone in the tribe was alerted; settlers and tribesmen alike searched the island for the beloved girl. But she had vanished and was presumed drowned in the sea. None of the people looking for the girl associated her disappearance with the appearance of a white deer that could sometimes be seen walking near the sound at dusk.

Only Okisko believed that she might still be alive. The grieving suitor spent many days in prayer and fasting, seeking knowledge of the lovely Virginia from the spirit world. On the afternoon of the third day, a brown pelican came to him on the winds of the sea and told him that Virginia had been transformed into a white deer by the black wizard Chico. The only way to free her was to pierce her heart with an arrow tipped by an oyster shell. Rejoicing in this good news, Okisko thanked the proud spirit of the brown pelican and immediately found an oyster shell, which he made into the head of an arrow.

Unbeknownst to Okisko, the evil Chico had revealed to one of the girl's rejected suitors—Wanchese—that the white deer grazing along the sound was none other than the missing Virginia Dare. Chico hoped that the jealous warrior would kill the doe, thus completing his revenge against the Englishwoman.

Wanchese hated the English who had settled among his people. Most especially did he hate Virginia Dare, who had favored Okisko's suit over his own. He had traveled to England with the first explorers and there had learned of a substance called silver that would kill the creatures created by black magic. Having some coins in his possession from that long-ago trip, he melted the metal in a hot fire and made an arrowhead of pure silver. As dusk fell over the island, Wanchese went hunting for the white deer down by the sound.

On the seaside of the island, the brown pelican flew urgently across the waves toward Okisko, who was affixing the oyster-shell tip to his arrow. "Hurry," the brown pelican called to him. "You must hurry. Another seeks for the white deer and would take her life!"

Okisko gasped in horror and ran across the island as fast as his strong body would carry him toward the place where the white deer had been seen walking beside the sound. As he reached the abandoned place where the City of Raleigh once stood, he saw the white deer walking down on the sandy shore. He took aim at once, the gleaming oyster-shell at the tip of his arrow, and shot the white deer in the heart. At the same moment, a silver-tipped arrow flew through the air from the far side of the clearing, and it too pierced the heart of the white deer.

The white deer gave a cry like that of a woman in pain. Its form shimmered, glowing so brightly that it blinded the eyes of the two warriors who had shot her. Then the light died away, and they saw, lying on the ground where the white deer had stood, the dying figure of beautiful Virginia Dare.

Okisko gave a wail of anguish and ran to his beloved's side. Behind him Wanchese laughed—an evil sound—and disappeared into the bracken—never to be seen again. Virginia Dare died in her beloved's arms and was buried in the old fort where her people had first settled. Okisko went on to become a great chief among his people, but he never married. His people whispered that the source of his success came from his spirit guide—a white deer who would appear sometimes to him at dusk down by the shores of the sound.

To this day, whenever a white deer appears along the shores of the Outer Banks, it is said that the spirit of Virginia Dare has returned to watch over the land that she once loved.

21

The Legend of Tsali

I watch over these high hills through the mist and the wind, the heat and the snow. I walk the deer paths over Clingman's Dome and wander the roadways and streams, drifting across the deep valleys at will. I guard my people and my land, as I have always done. As I always will. Most people who visit here never see me, and I am content that it be so. But to a chosen few who have the right eye and the right spirit, I appear with the dawn and the dusk, a Cherokee warrior whose spirit has never left his mountain home. As the sun sets over this high valley, I sit on an old stump at my favorite lookout and remember . . .

I remember that my people were forced to leave. In the end we had no choice. We had done everything the white men asked of us, adopting many of their ways, building roads and schools and churches. We even developed a system of representational government, and a brilliant Cherokee linguist named Sequoyah developed the written Cherokee alphabet—the Talking Leaves—without having any previous knowledge of a written script.

We were a people of peace. Many of us were farmers and cattle ranchers. But white settlers were rapidly filling the southern states, and the Cherokee lands—which extended from

Georgia to the Ohio River—were at the heart of the crossroads of commerce. This flood of settlers increased tensions between us and our white brothers. And then gold was found on Cherokee land. At that moment, the fate of our nation was sealed. In 1830 the Congress of the United States passed the Indian Removal Act, declaring that my people and many other tribes living in the South were to be sent away from the bones of our ancestors to live in Oklahoma Territory.

So we fought back. Not with spears and bows as we might once have fought. This time we used the laws of state and nation, up to the highest courts. And we won a reprieve, for the Supreme Court of the land said we were an independent nation and could not be removed unless a treaty was signed between ourselves and the U.S. government.

But the public tide was against us, even when the courts ruled in our favor. And soon some of the Cherokee were swayed to the side of removal, wearied by the long, hard battle against the U.S. government. And so they sold our birthright for $5 million and signed the Treaty of New Echota, giving President Andrew Jackson the legal document he needed to remove us from our lands.

Still, our advocates—like the statesman Davy Crockett—fought on our behalf. But the ratification of the treaty passed the Senate by one vote, and just like that, we lost our land. In May 1838 U.S. General Winfield Scott and his army invaded the Cherokee Nation, slashing and burning, seizing cattle, and thrusting families from their homes and into makeshift forts with minimal facilities and little food.

I was living in the Smoky Mountains in a small cabin with my wife and sons while the turmoil of politics raged in

THE LEGEND OF TSALI

Washington, D.C. I hunted and farmed the land and was far more concerned with the weather and my crops than with the goings-on of people who lived far away from my hills— that is, until my brother-in-law came for a visit to our cabin in May 1838 to tell us about the companies of soldiers who were searching the valleys of our home and herding thousands of Cherokee people into stockades in preparation for a great march to the west. It seemed fantastical to me at the time. How could such a thing be? But my brother-in-law was an honest man, and it must be so.

I was troubled as I returned to my fields to work. How would this impact my family? Would we be forced from our home in the hills of our ancestors? As I worked, sweat pouring down my back and legs, I saw in a flash a picture of my people living and working, laughing and crying and playing in these mountains many years into the future. They would be born here, wed here, die here, and would carry on the traditions and wisdom passed to us from our ancestors. I paused, stunned by this dream that had come to my mind. Was it possible? Could we resist this removal and win?

I made my way home when the work was done, still pondering my dream of the future. And shortly I found myself and my family confronted by white soldiers, who came to my cabin and ordered us to join the other Cherokee in the stockade at Bushnell. We were given little time to prepare for the journey and could take with us only the belongings we could carry.

All of us—myself, my wife, my sons, and my brother-in-law—left home under the guard of the soldiers. Outwardly, I was calm, and my stillness kept my sons calm. Inwardly, I was furious. How dare they force us off our land? I had signed no treaty. I had not even known there was a treaty until my brother-in-law had arrived. In front of me, my dear wife stumbled in fatigue, and one of the soldiers prodded her cruelly with his bayonet. I clenched my fists in rage and then spoke softly to my kinsmen in Cherokee, which the soldiers did not appear to understand. "When we reach the turn in the trail," I said to my sons, "I will trip and fall and complain of my ankle. When the soldiers stop, leap upon them and take their guns. Then we'll escape into the hills."

At the appropriate moment, I fell down on the path, miming an injury, and my sons leapt upon their captors with the help of my brother-in-law. In the short fracas that followed, a rifle went off, and one of the soldiers fell dead onto the forest floor. We fled then, knowing that the fury of the white men would follow us.

I led us up into the mountains to a concealed cave I knew of under the peak known as Clingman's Dome, knowing the white man's troops would be at a disadvantage in such a place, should they be able to track us this far. By the time we settled ourselves for the night, I knew that I would fight to the death rather than allow my family to become prisoners of the U.S. Army.

We lived as fugitives through the long summer that followed, foraging as best we could and avoiding the white soldiers who hunted us. Around us, the destruction continued, until the last band of Cherokee under the guardianship of U.S. soldiers left in the autumn for the west. It was at this time that Will Thomas, a white trader who had been adopted by a Cherokee chief, came to our cave on Clingman's Dome. He told us about the other Cherokee —numbering about a thousand—who had taken refuge in the mountains. Then he relayed a message from the U.S. General Scott, whose soldier had died in the fracas with my family: "If Tsali and his kin will come in and give up, I won't hunt down the others. If Tsali will voluntarily pay the penalty, I will intercede with the government to grant the fugitives permission to remain. But if Tsali refuses, I'll turn my soldiers loose to hunt every one of them."

We sat in silence in the cave, thinking about the general's words. Will Thomas looked into the fire, avoiding our eyes. In my mind I saw again that flash of vision I had in the field, the day I lost my farm: my people living and working, laughing and loving and dying in these mountains as they carried on the traditions and wisdom passed to us from our ancestors. I had shared this vision with my family, and as I looked from one face to another, I saw the same determination in each one. If our deaths could bring about such a future, how could we say no?

And so we turned ourselves in. I embraced my wife and wiped the tears from her eyes. Then we left our hiding place. We were met by a band of the Oconaluftee Cherokee who lived in Quallatown, those for whom our sacrifice would be made, and they brought us to the stockade. The trial was swiftly over. My son, my brother-in-law, and I were sentenced to die, but my wife and youngest son were spared. We were taken to the field next to the stockade and were stood against three trees. The colonel in charge asked us for our final words, and I said, "If I must be killed, I would like to be shot by my own people." I confess, I was surprised when they acceded to my request. Three Cherokee men were selected to be our executioners, and I saw in their faces that they understood the sacrifice we were making on behalf of our people. I glanced at my brother-in-law and at my brave son, who had lived so gallantly all his short life.

He gave me a nod, and we both looked into the barrels of the guns pointed at us, waving aside the offer of blindfolds. Then shots rang out in the valley, and our bodies fell to the earth, to be buried beside the stockade.

At that moment my spirit could have gone to be with my ancestors. My son and my brother-in-law certainly followed the sacred path before them. But I lingered behind in these mountains where I had lived and died. I wanted to watch over my wife and younger son. And I wanted to see whether our sacrifice made any difference for our people and whether the white man would keep his word.

And he did. The white man ruled that the Quallatown Cherokee who lived outside the official boundaries of the Cherokee Nation were not required by law to emigrate, and that those Cherokee still hiding in the mountains might join with them and live freely. And so the federal troops left our homeland . . .

And so I have remained, from that day to this, as a silent watcher over my people. We have grown in number through the years. Ten thousand Cherokee now live in the center of our ancient homeland. I guard their sleep and watch over their dreams as they live and work, laugh and love and die in these mountains and carry on the traditions and wisdom passed to us from our ancestors.

I stand, now and forever, at the soul and center of this land. My people call me Tsali.

22

Mercy

SMITHFIELD

The lieutenant had heard, of course, about the Union marauders following in the wake of General William Tecumseh Sherman, plundering houses, killing families, destroying what they did not steal. He had considered it despicable behavior and had spoken out against it, in the abstract. But the reality was not driven home to him until he walked into the ruins of his house in Smithfield and found both of his beloved parents dead at the hands of the most ruthless band of Union marauders that had ever pillaged the South.

As he buried his father—Confederate Colonel John Saunders—and his lovely, gentle mother in the family graveyard under a big tree, the lieutenant swore that he would exact vengeance against the men who had murdered them. And he knew exactly who they were. The David Fanning gang was fifty men strong, and they had been ransacking the countryside for months. Grimly, he went back to his commanding officer and requested a troop of men to help him track down the marauders. Sympathetic to his cause, the general granted his request.

For the next several weeks, the lieutenant and his men traveled through the countryside in search of the renegades.

But every lead petered out, every hint came to nothing. The lieutenant had never felt so frustrated in his life. The vision of his sweet mother's dead face was ever before his eyes, and the gruff voice of his father haunted his dreams at night. Surely, if there was a good God in heaven, justice must be done for these blameless, beloved folk!

There came a rustle from outside his door, and a soldier entered with an air of barely suppressed excitement. "They've been spotted, sir," he blurted out after the minimum of courtesies. "The marauders appear to have set up camp on an island in Hannah's Creek Swamp."

The lieutenant went very still as he absorbed the news. Hannah's Creek Swamp. He knew the place. It was remote, and the island at its center was a good place to hide. A flame of excitement swelled in his chest. Yes. This was it. He could feel it.

The young soldier eyed his commanding officer with concern. The lieutenant had not said a word since he made his report. Understanding the situation a little better, the older officer on duty at the door laid a hand on the lad's arm and gestured him quietly away. Then he went in to the lieutenant and asked for orders. The lieutenant looked up at last with fire in his eyes and ordered an immediate march on the swamp.

As they broke camp, the lieutenant realized that disguises would be necessary in order for them to safely reach the island without tipping off the marauders. When they reached Smithfield, they borrowed civilian clothing from the locals, who were happy to help the lieutenant sent to rescue them from David Fanning's band of killers.

Commandeering rowboats, the lieutenant set out across the swamp with his men. He stood in the lead boat and answered the hails from the island. "Union soldiers," he called when asked to identify himself. "We were forced out of the last county and heard there were Union soldiers near Smithfield. We are hoping to join your troop."

The leader of the marauders stepped to the edge of the shore and stared out at the disguised lieutenant. The eyes of the two men met, and the lieutenant's body stiffened as he realized he was looking at David Fanning, the man who had ordered the deaths of his parents. It took a great effort to keep his face still and calm.

"What unit?" Fanning called across the water.

"Sherman's XIV corps," the lieutenant called back with a grim smile, remembering how fiercely the Yankees in that corps had fought in the Battle of Bentonville.

Smiles broke out on the faces of the marauders, and they shouted welcomes to the men bearing down on them in boats. The lieutenant stepped ashore and came face-to-face with David Fanning.

"What's your name, brother?" Fanning asked jovially, holding out his hand.

"I am called John Saunders," the lieutenant said softly, refusing to take the outstretched hand. "Named for my father."

All around him, the Confederate soldiers' guns came up. The marauders were quickly surrounded and subdued. The color drained from Fanning's face as he recognized the name of Saunders.

"Search them," Saunders said grimly. He wanted no mistakes made in this raid. The men were searched, and Confederate plunder was found aplenty. And around the neck of Fanning himself was a crucifix of gold that the lieutenant had last seen adorning the neck of his beloved mother.

Enraged, he yanked the necklace from Fanning's neck and forced him to kneel with a gun to the back of his head. "You—all of you—are hereby found guilty of theft, marauding, and murder," the lieutenant said without emotion. Nodding to his sergeant, he said, "Hang them from the neck until they are dead."

The Confederate soldiers were quick to obey. Fanning gasped a protest, but a nudge from the gun at the back of his skull silenced him. Ropes were noosed around the necks of the marauders—fifty strong—and they were hauled up into the gnarled trees of the island in the swamp and hanged until they were dead.

Fanning, forced to kneel on the ground and watch his men die, alternated between angry curses and pleas for mercy. He was ignored.

When the last marauder was dead, Saunders ordered his men to the boats. They left the bodies of the Union soldiers hanging from the trees and dragged Fanning, tied hand and foot, into the lead boat. Then they force-marched the leader of the marauders back to Smithfield and down a familiar lane to an old family graveyard near the Saunderses' pillaged home.

When he saw the two brand-new gleaming white stones in the graveyard, Fanning dug in his heels and refused to walk a step farther. "Mercy," he gasped. "Mercy, I beg you." Then he looked into the lieutenant's eyes.

"Where was the mercy you showed when you stole this?" the lieutenant asked, holding up the gold crucifix. "The same mercy meted out by you is the mercy I offer you now."

MERCY

He nodded to his sergeant. "Hang him."

The sergeant nodded and looped a rope around David Fanning's neck. The marauder was hanged until he was dead from the tree growing above the graves of the elder Saunderses, his feet dangling over the gleaming white headstones.

The lieutenant stooped before his mother's grave and laid the crucifix tenderly on the stone. Justice was served. But somehow, it didn't make him feel any better. With his whole soul, he longed to see his mother one last time. To see her smile. To make her laugh.

He turned away and walked out of the graveyard as his men cut the dead Fanning down from the tree. Justice. Mercy. Duty. Revenge. The lieutenant was sick of it all. He just wanted to go home.

For years after the Southern surrender in Yorktown, rumors circulated about the Hannah's Creek ghosts. Folks wandering through the swamp or boating on the small lake claimed they could hear pleas for mercy and see ghostly bodies hanging from the gnarled trees. Such was its reputation that people started avoiding the place, until it was completely reclaimed by the wilderness and the island was swallowed up by the swamp. But they say if you roam near Hannah's Creek at night, you can still hear David Fanning pleading for mercy as his men are strung up on ghostly, gnarled trees that no longer exist.

23

Jubilee

VANDEMERE

Boom! Boom! Boooom!

My twelve-year-old daughter Hannah and I were sitting down to a belated afternoon lunch when we were startled by a massive thunderclap of sound like the booming of cannon.

Boooom!

My seven-year-old son Jason, who had eaten earlier, shot into the kitchen with a yell of sheer delight: "Jubilee! Jubilee!"

He grabbed my hand and tried to pull me out of my chair, shouting, "Come on, Mom!"

Hannah whooped and jumped out of her chair, her glass of milk tumbling to the floor behind her. "I'll get the tongs and the shovels," Hannah yelled, blonde hair wild about her face as she pounded out of the kitchen, heading for the back hall closet.

My husband, Carl, flew into the kitchen next. "Nets! Marie, where are the nets?"

"In the garage where they always are," I said, a calm center in the midst of chaos. I calmly took another sip of coffee as I shooed Jason and Carl toward the garage.

Boom! Boom!

Like our neighbors to the south, we Vandemere folk sometimes hear the loud reporting of the "Seneca Guns." The sound is a mystery. As sharp and echoing as cannon fire, it vibrates up and down the coast, startling everyone who hears it. Doors and windows tremble and reverberate in sympathy when it starts, adding to the racket. No one can trace its source or discover why it happens. It has baffled scientists for years, but we locals have grown accustomed to it over the decades and simply call it the Seneca Guns.

In Vandemere the sound of the Seneca Guns triggers a second natural phenomenon: the Jubilee. Nobody really knows why the Jubilee comes with the sound of the Seneca Guns. But we are sure glad it does. A Jubilee occurs when many species of crab and shrimp, as well as flounder, eels, and other fish, leave deeper waters and congregate—in large numbers and very high density—in the shallow waters by the shore. First, minnows and small fish race toward the shore as if they were trying to beach themselves. They are rapidly followed by larger fish, crabs, and sometimes even scallops. For about an hour, the shallow waters teem with sea creatures of all kinds while the Seneca Guns boom. But the harvest is so plentiful that we are still eating from it a month later.

Scientists say that a Jubilee occurs when deeper parts of the sound undergo a rapid depletion of oxygen, which drives fish to the surface seeking oxygenated water. But that doesn't explain why such low levels of oxygen start whenever the Seneca Guns sound, or stop when the Seneca Guns stop.

Boom! Boom! Boooom!

In the back bedroom my two-year-old son Chris started wailing softly, wakened from his nap by all the noise and confusion. Outside I could hear the neighbors calling to one another as they grabbed baskets, buckets, shovels, tongs, whatever they could get their hands on to help with the harvest. Everyone in town knew what it meant when the Seneca Guns started booming in Vandemere.

"Crab walk!" I heard someone yell in the road out front.

"Time of Jubilee!" came the answer from my neighbor across the street.

Boom went the Seneca Guns up and down the coast. The noise was so loud that it rattled the windows in the nursery. Little Chris held his arms up to me as I reached his bed. I swept him up, feeling a lump in my throat. The last time the Seneca Guns had boomed along this coast, my mother was still alive. She had watched little Chris while the rest of us ran down to the beach for the harvest. But Mom was dead now—passed in her sleep from a silent heart attack. I didn't relish taking my two-year-old into the chaos on the beach, but I couldn't leave him behind. And Hannah was old enough to help watch him while we harvested shrimp and crabs and fish from the teeming waters.

It took five minutes to get everything assembled. Pulling Chris in a small wagon filled with a cooler and several baskets, I followed my family out into the bustling streets, joining the dancing, singing, exclaiming crowd headed to the shore.

Boom! Boom! Boooom!

By the time we arrived, the shallows were boiling with fish. Crabs scuttled from the shallows to the shore, and then back into the shallows. I could see scallops jetting back and forth like small torpedoes under the lapping waves.

Jason and Hannah raced into the water in their cutoffs and old sneakers and started pitching fish into a basket they had jammed in the doughnut hole of an automobile inner tube. Carl was after crabs—his favorite—netting them carefully and tossing them into a cooler. People thronged the beach, enthusiastically wading into the water with crab nets and tongs and shovels. Children raced around in circles and splashed themselves silly, parents shouted instructions, and old fishermen calmly netted the largest fish. Chaos surrounded us, and the noise level made my ears ring, but it was great fun just the same!

Boom! Boooom!

In the shallows, submerged in a few inches of water, crabs were stacked up in rows as dense as cars in a parking lot. There were a lot of fish species too: small fish and flounder struggling along at the edge where tiny waves lapped the shore, their upper gill covers literally rising into the air in a desperate search for oxygen.

Little Chris wiggled and wiggled in my arms, wanting to wade into the water with his brother and sister. Hannah, seeing my dilemma, shouted, "It's okay, Mom. I'll watch him. You go help Dad."

She shoved aside a couple of gasping flounder and took him from my arms. I smiled in relief. Chris was getting heavy now that he was two. I was really thankful for that babysitting class Hannah took last year. It was worth every blessed penny we paid.

I grabbed for one of the shovels and scooped it under a flounder, heaving it into the cooler with Carl's crabs. Flounder was *my* favorite meal. And I wanted to scoop up some of those scallops before my next-door neighbor cornered the market.

Boom! Boom! Boooom! The Seneca Guns were still vibrating up and down the coastline, eclipsing even the noise of the crowd.

Suddenly, Hannah was beside me, dripping wet and pale with fright. "Mom! Mom! I can't find Chris!"

I dropped my shovel into the water, and it disappeared under the silvery streaks of thousands of minnows. "What do you mean you can't find Chris!" I shouted, panic ripping through me, my eyes already scanning the crowded shoreline.

Hannah was fighting back tears. "He was holding my hand, and we were wading at the edge of the water when I tripped over a stone and fell into the water right on top of a huge crab. I must have dropped Chris's hand when I fell, because I couldn't find him anywhere when I got back on my feet!"

"You go tell your father and brother. I'll start searching," I gasped through a tight throat. "Where were you when you fell?"

Hannah pointed to the spot and then ran down the beach toward Carl. I raced in the opposite direction, toward the spot where my baby had disappeared, bumping into neighbors, friends, and children running back and forth to baskets and buckets and coolers on the beach, their nets full of flopping fish and scuttling crabs. I asked everyone about Chris. No one had seen him. Many people broke off their harvesting to help me search the shallows. The body of a small boy could easily be hidden under the teeming fish in the water. My heart clenched at the morbid thought, and I shook it off. Chris was fine. He had to be!

Boom! Boooom! The Seneca Guns roared their mysterious message up and down the beach.

And then I saw a familiar little figure in tiny khaki shorts and a white T-shirt. He was walking up the beach toward me, holding the hand of an elderly woman in a flower-print dress. I froze in shock, recognizing the woman at once. My heart

JUBILEE

thudded painfully against my ribs, and I broke into a cold sweat, unable to take my eyes off the woman's laughing face. It was my dead mother!

Chris was chuckling and pointing at the fish squirming their way out of the water. My mother was saying the name of each kind of fish he pointed to. Neither of them saw me. Then Chris looked past a couple of kids hauling a large flounder out of the shallows by its gills and saw me.

"Mommy," he shouted. Dropping my mother's hand, he ran to me and flung his arms around my legs. My knees gave way, and I fell onto the hard, wet sand, clutching him close while tears poured down my cheeks. All the time, I stared up at my mother, who was wearing her favorite flower-print dress that we'd buried her in. She smiled at me lovingly, just as she had in life. And then she was gone, just like that.

A moment later I felt Carl's arms close around me. He was shaking with relief. Then Hannah and Jason piled on top of us, nearly toppling me to the ground. A crab scuttled past us, heading up the beach as fast as it could. I hardly noticed.

Boooom! The sound was fainter now, fading away. And the fish were not so plentiful in the shallows. The scallops had already jetted away, and the fish were following. We helped each other up, clinging together gratefully. Hannah was frantic with sorrow, apologizing again and again. Finally, Carl picked her up like he had when she was a little girl. "You didn't mean to fall," he said, wiping away her tears. "Chris could have gotten away from any of us in this crowd. It's all right now."

"Hannah cry," Chris observed with concern.

"Hannah will be okay in a minute," I told him. Jason trotted along beside us, wordless with relief. Then he spotted our abandoned baskets and raced forward to claim them before they went home with another family. Carl put Hannah down and shooed her after Jason. I clung tightly to Chris as my husband and children gathered up our tools and the baskets and cooler full of crabs, scallops, and other bounty from the sea. It was time to go home.

I packed Chris in among the filled baskets and pushed him home in the wagon. All the time I thought about what I had seen on the beach. My mother—my dead mother—had rescued her grandson when he became lost in the crowd. It seemed impossible. But that was what I'd seen.

Mom had looked younger than she had when I last saw her. And she looked happy, for which I was thankful. I bent toward my young son and whispered, "Who did you see at the beach, Chris?" Chris, his fingers tightly curled around the handle of the cooler, looked up with a grin. "Grammy," he said. "I see Grammy!"

My heart contracted inside me, with the pain of my mother's loss combined with the joy of seeing her one more time. The lump in my throat was so huge that I couldn't speak. I just brushed my baby's hair from his forehead and looked across the wagon at Carl. I'd tell him about Mom when we got home, I decided. Right now, I was too filled up with joy and relief to say a word. I just smiled at my family, thanking God for a beautiful summer day and a successful Jubilee.

24

Raven Mockers

CHEROKEE

He woke out of a sound sleep, trembling from head to toe, unsure what had caused him to wake. The house was silent except for the soft breathing of his wife. And outside the walls, a strange hush lay over the world. Save for the soft whisper of the wind, there were no sounds at all. He kept waiting for the stealthy rustle of a passing fox, the grunt of a bear, the soft whisper of an owl's wings. But there was nothing.

Then he heard the sharp, unmistakable cry of a diving raven. He knew then what had awakened him. The Raven Mockers were gathering. Which meant that someone in the village was dying. He broke into a cold sweat, rising swiftly and fumbling into his clothes. His wife rolled over without waking as he grabbed for his bow and headed out the door. Who was sick? Who was dying? No one had reported an illness, though he had noticed old Galilani, a Beloved Woman of the tribe, had a bad cough when he last saw her. Beloved Woman was a prestigious title given to extraordinary women by the Cherokee clans. Galilani headed the Council of Women, held a voting seat in the Council of Chiefs, and had responsibility over prisoners. She was an important person in their village. Too important to lose to the Raven Mockers.

He paused on his doorstep, trying to orient himself. Then he saw the fiery shapes floating overhead, arms outstretched like wings and sparks trailing behind them. Yes, they were headed east, toward the house where old Galilani lived with her widowed daughter. He ran then, as fast as he had ever run. The witches would torment their victim, frightening her, throwing her to the floor, and pummeling her until she died. Then they would remove the heart of their victim and eat it, adding all the hours and days she might have survived to their own lives. And no one in the house would know about it, for the Raven Mockers could make themselves invisible.

He was one of the few medicine men who could see the Raven Mockers in their invisible form, and so he was always called to attend the sick and dying to help keep the witches away. Not knowing what he would find when he reached the house, he pulled one of the special arrows he saved for such witches from his quiver so that it would be ready.

Yes, there was a light on. He ran to the door, knocking and entering at the same time. It was a small, one-room cabin, and the widowed daughter was bent over a small bed where her mother lay. She was surrounded by withered creatures outlined in fire, their gnarled hands poking and prodding the still figure on the bed. The daughter turned when she heard someone enter the room. Her eyes widened when she saw him in the doorway with an arrow already nocked. But she understood at once what it meant.

"Drop," he told her, his voice tight but calm. She fell to the floor, and he shot his magic arrow straight at the closest Raven Mocker. It screamed and writhed in agony as the arrow pierced its heart. Then it vanished in a cloud of sparks, and he

RAVEN MOCKERS

knew its foul spirit had returned to its body far away. The other Raven Mockers wailed when they saw the medicine man in their midst. Generally, they hid from such holy men. The evil spells that dominated the life of a Raven Mocker dictated that for the witch to be effective, he or she must live in disguise. If a Raven Mocker was recognized in its human guise, the spells would turn against it, and he or she would die within a week. And holy men, such as the medicine man, were notoriously good at spotting a Raven Mocker in human form once they have seen its spirit.

Only one witch remained calm as the medicine man rapidly nocked a second arrow. Staying focused, it slapped the old woman so hard on the face that her neck snapped, and she fell back dead. The medicine man's second arrow pierced the heart of the killer, but the witch beside it pulled out a flaming knife and slipped it between the old woman's ribs. His third arrow killed the witch before it could cut out the Beloved Woman's heart, and his fourth arrow eliminated another. Each disappeared in a shower of sparks.

The widowed daughter sprawled on the floor, staring from the grim medicine man to the bed where her dead mother lay. She could see the magic arrows flying through the air and then vanishing, but nothing more. The assembled Raven Mockers remained invisible to her eyes.

Overwhelmed by the ferocity of the medicine man's attack, the remaining Raven Mockers dispersed, trailing their fiery way straight through the walls and ceilings of the cabin. The medicine man gasped with relief as the last of them disappeared, and then he strode forward to offer the daughter a hand up. Reading in his face that the danger was over, she fled to the bed and fell weeping upon her dead mother.

"It happened so quickly," she told the medicine man. "She just had a bad cough until this evening. She woke up gasping for breath about an hour ago, and I was so busy attending her that I had no time to send for you."

"Pneumonia," he said, quietly closing the old woman's eyes. "At least the Raven Mockers did not take her heart."

They would have to watch over the body now until burial, or the Raven Mockers would return. Once the old woman was buried, her heart was safe. He sent the widowed daughter to call for her brother and his spouse to join their vigil. At dawn he sent a message to his wife so that she would not be frightened by his sudden absence. Then he arranged a quick burial for Galilani, since she had almost been taken by Raven Mockers.

The whole village turned out to bid farewell to the Beloved Woman, who had been a favorite of many. The medicine man stood silent watch over the proceedings and thought about the Raven Mockers he had marked with his arrows. The witches had come swiftly to torture their victim when she fell ill. So they could not live far away. He was shaken by the number of them. He had counted six witches by the old woman's bedside, and of those he had marked four with his arrows. Now, watching the grief of the family at the unexpected passing of their mother, he felt determination rise within him. No more would these evil witches harm his people or shorten their lives. He was going raven hunting.

He was confident he could find the four he had shot with his magic arrows. He would have to trust that the spirits would guide him to the other two.

The medicine man consulted briefly with the council elders after the burial. His strong medicine was known to them, and they approved of his plan to rid the tribe of the local witches. With their blessing he set off on his self-appointed task.

First, he spent two days in the sweat lodge, praying and seeking wisdom for his hunt. Then he set out with his magic arrows, his knife, and a rifle for more ordinary hunting. He circled the village once, twice, seeking signs of the Raven Mockers' recent passage through the air. The spirit sparks that followed them surely must have injured more than one tree. Praying for the keen eyesight of the eagle and the agility of the squirrel, he climbed several likely-looking tall trees. On the third one he found the small char marks for which he searched.

Dropping back to the ground, he followed the overgrown trail beneath it for more than an hour, until he found a small cabin tucked away into a hollow in the mountain. A middle aged man was chopping wood behind the cabin, and a woman was doing laundry by the stream bed that passed through one corner of the hollow. It was a perfectly ordinary scene. But the medicine man could see more. His spirit sight perceived the red glow coming through the man's rough shirt in the region of his heart. At the medicine man's side, the magic arrows glowed in response. Then the woman turned, and he saw a similar red glow at her shoulder. Aha! The spirits were with him. He had found two Raven Mockers less than an hour from the village. Nocking an arrow, he stepped into the clearing.

The man and woman looked up at his approach. They recognized him at once, and fear twisted their faces. For a moment all the extra time they had stolen from their victims sat upon their countenances, turning them withered and old and twisted. Then they fled the clearing while he rained arrows after them. He didn't bother to kill them. He'd seen the truth in their faces and knew the witches were doomed. He could hear the woman weeping as she fled.

It took the medicine man two more days to find the next Raven Mocker. He was nearing a local village when he heard the familiar raven screech and heard the strong wind that accompanied it. Sparks were shooting through the roof of a local house.

"Raven Mocker," he shouted to a few men walking the path near him. He was well known in this village for his gift of medicine sight, and the men instantly followed him toward the house. The local holy man was already there, glaring defiantly around the room with sacred objects held ready in his hands. He did not have the same gift of sight as the medicine man, but his holy senses knew that danger was near. He nodded welcome to the men in the doorway as he stood guard over the little child in the cradle that was the Raven Mocker's object.

The medicine man nocked his magic arrows, watching from the doorway. Then he let fly, and the magic arrow shot straight through the throat of the Raven Mocker lurking near the hearth. It disappeared in a shower of sparks. Instantly he followed the sparks, seeing the witch's spirit rise above the treetops as it fled back to its body. A mile down the path, the medicine man found a wrinkled old man crouched over a tiny fire within a circle of evergreens. He sat so still that he might have been dead, but the medicine man knew better. He saw the flaming spirit of the Raven Mocker descending through the sky toward the body. But he had found it first. He sent a magic arrow through the heart of the old man. As the dead body tumbled to the ground, the witch's spirit burst into flames in midair and disappeared.

The medicine man returned in triumph to the village with the body of the witch, and they buried him deep beneath a stone. There was great rejoicing in the village, for the witch had been menacing and dominating them for many years, and no one had been able to touch him until that day. The village elders begged him to stay and eat with them, but the medicine man had three more Raven Mockers to track and slay, and so he wished them well and continued his journey.

The medicine man found the fourth Raven Mocker by sheer luck more than a week after he left his home. She was cunningly hidden in a cave near the outskirts of a small village way down in the valley. The villagers knew nothing of her presence, but people in the vicinity reported that the number of sudden or surprising deaths had significantly increased over the past two years. The elders had suspected the presence of a Raven Mocker but had been unable to locate it. The medicine man himself would have missed her, for she was a clever shape-shifter, but he had seen his arrow mark pulsing in her neck when she passed him, disguised as a local tribeswoman. There were too many people about for him to kill her at the time. Instead, he went to the village elders and told them what he had seen. Then he tracked the Raven Mocker back to her lair with two of the best hunters in the village.

One look into their eyes was enough to tell the withered old Raven Mocker that she was discovered. Before any of the men could react, the witch fell on her own knife rather than die at their hands.

"Bury her deep," the medicine man instructed the elders before departing again on his search.

He was gone more than a month from his home, but he did not find the two remaining Raven Mockers living in the region.

Admitting defeat at last, he returned home to his welcoming wife and reluctantly told the council of elders how he had fared.

"Four fewer witches to worry us?" they said to him. "You consider this defeat? Well done!"

They told him that the bodies of the male and female Raven Mockers he found the first day had been washed up in the stream in his absence. They were buried deep under a stone in a field outside the village.

The medicine man was uneasy and restless after returning to his home. He went about his daily tasks in an abstracted manner. The task still felt undone. But the remaining Raven Mockers were warned now of his sworn vengeance, and they did not appear in the village, even when two children came down with a high fever. Not a whoosh of wind or a raven scream did he hear, though he watched beside their beds for a day and a night.

He was preparing to leave the children's house on the morning of the third day, assuring their mother that they were both out of danger and would be fine with a few days' rest, when their young father returned home from his weeklong hunting trip. He was wild-eyed and panting as he burst into the room. "Raven Mockers," he gasped to the medicine man. "Two of them."

The medicine man's eyes widened in triumph. "Where? Tell me!"

Dropping into a crouch to ease the ache in his side, the hunter related his story. Dusk had overtaken him one night far from any village, but he had remembered seeing a house not far from the trail where an old man and his wife lived. No one was home when he arrived, so he had curled up in a corner and gone to sleep. He was awakened late at night by the cry of a raven, and a moment later the old man came in and built a fire. The young hunter found something menacing in the scene and had remained still and silent as the old man took something out of a bundle and began roasting it over the coals. It looked like a man's heart.

Shortly thereafter, there came another sharp raven cry from outside, and then an old woman came in, frowning fiercely. "Did you have any luck?" her husband asked genially.

"None at all. There were too many holy men about," the woman grumbled.

"You never have any luck. Here, finish roasting this, and we will eat."

The woman bent over the fire for a time and then raised her head sharply. "Who is over in that corner?" she asked her husband.

"No one was there when I entered," he replied.

"And how would you know in the dark?" she asked. Rapidly they built up the fire. Alarmed, the young hunter feigned deep sleep, not responding to the loud noise they made at the fire, and only opening his eyes when the old man shook him. He rubbed his face and head and pretended great weariness as he spoke to his host.

Ignoring him, the wife hurried outside into the gray of predawn, and the young hunter heard her crying. He knew she was frightened because he might have overheard their conversation and identified them as Raven Mockers. If he had, their evil magic would turn against them, and they would perish. The young man hurried through the breakfast the old woman had prepared and exited the house as hastily as he could. The old man, hoping to bribe the hunter to forget anything he might have overheard, gave him a fancy piece of beadwork and a trumped-up explanation for his quarrel with the wife. At the next stream the hunter had thrown the beadwork away and had raced for home as fast as his legs would carry him.

He had traveled three and a half days since leaving that house, running as fast as he could, to summon the medicine men and the other tribal warriors. And they traveled three and a half days back to the place where the two remaining Raven Mockers lived.

It was exactly seven nights after the young hunter had overheard the Raven Mockers roasting a man's heart when the execution party reached their door. And true to their nature, the old man and woman lay dead on the floor of their house, killed by the evil spells that had once ruled them.

The medicine man ordered them burned with the entirety of their house and belongings. Then the hunters returned home, rejoicing that all the Raven Mockers in the range of their settlement had been destroyed.

Word of the medicine man who killed Raven Mockers spread throughout the Cherokee Nation. And Gunskali 'ski, the man who saw the invisible, was often called upon to sit with the sick and the dying and to hunt Raven Mockers from that day forward.

25

The Cat

EDENTON

I knew she was a witch the moment I laid eyes on her. At the time, I sat on the earthen dam beside my papa's mill with a fishing rod in my hand, and my mind on a tricky math problem I was trying to solve for school the next day. Then my eyes caught movement on the far side of the lake, and I saw the witch floating across the large millpond in a boat with no oars. There was no wind or stream to propel the boat forward, yet forward it came through the spring dusk that had fallen beneath the cyprus trees that surrounded our mill. The far side of the pond was a tangled forest dense with trees and underbrush. It was a darkly mysterious place, and no one ventured there because of the rumors that evil forces roamed the woods at night. Yet it was from this spot that the woman came to us in her magic boat.

Papa stood a few yards down from me, trying to catch us a catfish for dinner. He was watching the boat float toward us, but he didn't seem to notice that it had no oars or other means of propulsion. I thought his calm attitude strange at the time, not realizing he was already under the witch's spell.

In those days I was a precocious eleven-year-old tomboy with brains too big for my head, as Papa was fond of saying. I

173

THE CAT

was in the advanced class at school, and my teacher told Papa I had a better vocabulary than a politician and ought to go to high school as soon as I reached a suitable age. In spite of my academic achievements, I spent all my free time running about in britches and ragtag flannel shirts with the sleeves rolled up, my brown hair hanging in two long braids over each shoulder. It was not uncommon for us to go fishing together, and sometimes Papa took me hunting too. Perhaps these were not womanly pursuits, but I had never cared about that—until the moment when the witch drew near the shore, and I saw her beautiful face under a stylish poke bonnet and beheld the wonderful dress she wore. I was filled instantly with jealousy. We could never afford such fancy clothing, even when the mill was working to capacity. My only dress was a worn gingham that was two sizes too small. I glared unhappily down at my britches and patched shirt, comparing them unfavorably with the witch's garb.

Then I forgot all about my clothes. Papa had stepped forward to help the woman ashore, and he looked like a stricken spaniel, all wide pleading eyes. He stammered when he spoke to her, and his face by turns went white and then flushed a bright red.

The witch spoke in a low, musical voice, explaining that she had journeyed a long way and lost her husband on the trip. She asked if we knew of a place she could spend the night. Judging from the look in Papa's eyes, I knew what his answer would be even before he spoke. He quickly offered up our cottage as a resting place, and she delicately accepted. Then, as an afterthought, he introduced me. We stared at each other for a moment, the witch and I. From the disdainful curl of her upper lip, I judged that she disapproved of my clothes. But she said all the right things, and Papa glared at me until I gave her a polite—if sullen—greeting.

The witch—who said her name was Faye—insisted on cooking dinner for us in exchange for our hospitality. Papa followed her every move with his stricken-spaniel look, taking in her glossy black hair, her red lips, her amber-colored eyes, and her hourglass figure. She smiled beguilingly at him as she served up his stew, and she laughed at his remarks even when he was not funny at all. It was a sickening display, but Papa lapped it up. When Faye came to put stew in my bowl, I flinched away. I couldn't help it. I already hated her for the spell she seemed to have over Papa. She glared at me, yellow sparks glowing in her amber eyes. But her red mouth kept smiling. Our eyes met for a moment, and in them I could see the future plainly. She was going to be my new mama, and God help me if I tried to interfere. She had years of experience and black magic on her side, and I was just a simple miller's daughter.

As Papa and Faye conversed that first evening, I wondered why she was bothering with him. He was a simple man, rough of speech and manner. His interests mainly lay in fishing and milling, and he did not get out much or care for the world outside our small town. Faye was well-spoken, well-read, and well-bred. They truly had nothing in common. But Faye wanted him, and that was that.

One night's stay turned into two, then three. A week passed. Then a month. And when the itinerant preacher made his stop in our town, Papa and Faye were married.

Things weren't too bad at first. Faye was polite to me when Papa was around, and when he worked in the mill, she ignored me. I was not important in her grand scheme of things, whatever that was. Of course, many of my daylight hours were spent in the local school, wearing my hated gingham dress and learning all the things Papa could not teach me—for his knowledge of academics was limited to the basic accounting and writing needed for his job at the mill. So I had no idea what Faye did during the hours I was away. But at nighttime she was coldly polite to me and cuddled in a sickeningly sweet manner with Papa.

I found it rather annoying to be considered so unimportant. Faye didn't even try to hide her magic from me when I returned each day from school. I'd swing through the cottage door with my heavy load of schoolbooks and find the broom sweeping itself across the floor or the laundry flying in through the window to fold itself neatly away in the dresser drawers. Faye would be preening herself in the small mirror she'd placed over our fireplace mantel the day she and Papa were married. She could not get enough of her own reflection and was as vain of her appearance as a pussycat. I would sit down at the kitchen table and do my homework while she languidly started dinner. The fire would burst into flame without her lifting a finger, and food would fly this way and that, chopping itself, setting itself into a pot or frying pan. But the magic always stopped abruptly a minute or two before Papa came home, and Faye would be bustling around the stove each night when the front door opened to admit her infatuated husband. Secretly, I rather admired the beautiful witch. I'd like to be able to command inanimate objects to perform for me. But having a good Christian upbringing, I knew that some evil price had to be paid for her to have gained such power. And I wasn't sure I wanted to pay such a price just to avoid housework.

I'm not sure when the change began. One morning, Faye had a hard time getting out of bed, and I was forced to fix breakfast for Papa and myself before leaving for school. Papa fretted that Faye was sickening for something, but to my jaundiced eye it looked as if Faye had gone out late at night and not returned until dawn. In that moment I got an inkling of why Faye had married my father. His mill was ideally situated at the edge of the great woods where the evil witches and other dark creatures were said to conduct their grim deeds. She could easily participate in nightly revels and have a warm, comfortable, safe place to lodge during the day.

I said nothing to Papa of my speculations. I'd tried to tell Papa that he had married a witch, but he had scolded me soundly and had threatened to thrash me if I spoke such things in the town. So I kept my mouth shut. He was too far gone under Faye's spell to believe a word I said.

Around midsummer Papa went away on a hunting trip and insisted that Faye and I stay at the neighbors' farm until he returned. This was not a good idea. Within a day or two of our arrival, I overheard the neighbor's wife telling her husband that Faye's bed had only a small, cat-size hollow in the mattress when she went to make it each morning after breakfast, rather than the large hollow typically made by a full-grown human. The husband and wife exchanged significant looks when she said this, but they spoke no more of the matter at the time, for Faye chose that moment to trip happily into the room with a huge bouquet of flowers in her arms, freshly picked from the fields outside the farm.

Several times during that visit, I heard Faye creeping out of the farmhouse at night. She never returned before dawn. The farmer's wife heard her too, and she nodded significantly to her husband when Faye missed breakfast two days in a row and spent most of the afternoon napping. They looked pityingly at me, and the farmer—a round, jolly old man with a shock of white hair, a broad red face, and peppermints in his pockets—told me that I was welcome to stay at their house anytime, should the need arise. That was as far as they would go in expressing their opinion of my father's wife. At least to me. In town they were far more candid. By the time Papa arrived home from his trip, everyone in Edenton was convinced that he had married a witch.

Papa was furious when the rumors reached his ears. He would not believe me when I told him that I had nothing to do with the "vicious talk," and he thrashed me soundly with a willow switch until I could not sit down at supper. He wouldn't speak to me that night, or for much of the following week, as business at the mill slacked off because of the rumors. In the house Faye spent much of the day sleeping, becoming her vivacious self only after the evening meal. And she neglected the chores— not even bothering to clean with her magic. I found myself cooking and cleaning and doing any number of housewifely tasks just to keep our little home running.

Meanwhile, things at the mill were going wrong for Papa. The grinding wheels that mashed the grain to powder started sparking and jerking strangely, and he had to stop his work to fix them. The next day, he found nails in the grain hopper. And the day after that, he found many sacks of corn slashed open and grain spilled everywhere. Papa scolded me furiously that evening, sure that my "nasty talk" had encouraged the neighbors to play tricks on him. I cowered away from him, afraid of my own father for the first time in my life. His rough face was dark red and contorted with anger. Surprisingly, it was Faye herself who intervened, saying languidly, "What does it matter, my dear? We are above such childish tricks. Who cares if the peasants talk?"

Her words mollified my father, at least long enough for me to escape outdoors. My shaking legs took me down the lane to the farmer's house without my mind engaging in a conscious choice. The farmer's wife saw me coming and flung the door wide so that she could embrace me, murmuring soothing words until my sobs had ceased. Her husband hovered protectively around us, and he pressed several peppermints into my hands and called me his good girl as I poured out my woeful tale. I told them everything—from Faye's arrival in the magic boat to my beating and the terrible things happening at Papa's mill. If I was going to be blamed for all the witch talk in town, then I may as well talk!

The farmer's wife urged her husband to speak to Papa on my behalf, and he agreed to do so the very next day. Reassured by their calm manner, I wiped my eyes, ate some peppermints, and went home. It was dark when I arrived home, and the house was empty. Papa's absence was easily explained. He always went to the country store to play checkers with the other men on Wednesday evenings. But Faye was usually home.

I went over to the fire and added a few logs and then lit the lantern. Outside, the wind had sprung up, and I heard the growl of thunder. A storm was coming. I listened uneasily as the thunder grew nearer and the wind grew louder. I went to fetch the sweater I was knitting for Papa and tried to concentrate on it, but I kept dropping stitches. I kept wondering if the dam gate was open. A sudden storm such as this one might cause flooding, and that could easily wash out the mill. With Papa away at the country store and Faye gone to whatever witches' Sabbath she attended at night, it was up to me to protect the mill.

A sudden downpour thundered against the roof of the cottage. I shuddered with dread at the sound. If this kept up, the mill *would* be in danger. I shrugged into my coat and hurried outside with my lantern. I was instantly drenched, and the wind howled so fiercely around me that I staggered, the light of the lantern bobbing wildly in my hand. And that's when I saw the black cats swarming around the door of the mill. There were more than a dozen of them, and they were huge cats—almost the size of cougars—with blazing eyes and bristling tails. They batted at the mill door with giant paws until it fell open. I gaped at them. They must be witches' familiars, I decided. But why were they interested in our mill? I could see through the open doorway and realized that they were circling around something in the mill. What mischief were the creatures planning?

I crept cautiously to the closest window, rose on tiptoe, and looked inside. To my horror, I saw my father standing in the center of a rapidly tightening circle of giant black cats. He hadn't gone to the country store at all. He had been lying in wait for the vandals who were sabotaging the mill. And he had found more than he had bargained for.

The huge cats swiped at him with their long claws. I saw bloody tears in his shirt, and one leg of his pants was hanging down in back, nearly ripped off by a black cat with blazing amber eyes. As I watched, Papa swung at it desperately with his axe.

There was no way he could hold them all off on his own, I realized, glancing around for a weapon I could use to help defend my father. Seeing a long stick on the nearby woodpile, I grabbed it and charged toward the door of the mill.

At that moment, there came a tremendous caterwauling from inside. I was knocked sprawling by a dozen wailing cats that came bursting through the mill door. They were followed a moment later by my father, who dropped his axe into the mud as he clutched the doorpost for balance. He was dazed and injured. I rolled upright, intent on reaching him and helping him to safety. But he revived suddenly and staggered down the path toward the cottage. I shouted to him, but my call was drowned out by the thunderous rain. So I raced after him, fighting the rain and the heavy wind. Please God, let him be all right!

As I slammed open the front door, I heard Papa shout with horror from his bedroom. I gasped and ran toward the bedroom door. Then I froze in shock. Papa was staring disbelievingly at Faye, who lay bleeding on the bed. One of her arms had been severed at the wrist. "You!" he cried in a voice of such anguish that it wrung my heart. "You were the cat with the amber eyes that injured me? You, who I took into my heart and into my home?"

"Yes, me, you silly fool. Me! Why else would I stay with such a common fellow as you, except to be near my brethren?" Faye screamed. And she transformed suddenly into a huge black cat with blazing amber eyes and leapt at him, sharp claws extending from her three remaining paws. Papa dodged out of the way, and I ducked as the witch cat leapt right over me and raced out the front door.

Papa turned to stare at me, his eyes huge with horror. "Oh, little girl! Oh, my baby. I'm so sorry," he gasped. "I beat you, and all the time you were telling me the truth."

Tears sprang to my eyes. Papa already looked different, as if the witch's spell had been broken at last. I reached out to him, and he swept me into his arms, apologizing over and over for bringing Faye into our house.

It was at this moment that we both heard a sudden watery roar from the stream that fed the millpond. We'd heard that terrible sound once before, and it had nearly destroyed our mill. It was a flash flood!

My eyes widened. "Papa! I didn't have time to open the dam gate. I was distracted by the black cats!"

"Stay here," Papa said quickly. "I'll go."

"But you're injured," I shouted after him. He was already gone through the open door into the pounding rain. I raced after him, ignoring his injunction. His legs were much longer than mine, and he quickly outdistanced me. I saw him run out along the dam; saw the huge wave of water hit it; saw the dam shudder with the impact and dissolve into nothingness, throwing my father into the swirling nightmare of the flash flood.

I screamed. I ran along the bank of the pond, searching desperately for a glimpse of my father. I saw nothing but swirling, muddy water and the debris from the dam. Finally, I ran down the lane, bursting in on the sleeping farmer and his wife, shouting desperately for assistance. The farmer came at once, while his wife roused the other neighbors.

Everyone searched along the shore of the large pond in the pouring rain, the bravest venturing on the side closest to the witch woods. The pond had overflowed its banks in the flash flood, making the search difficult. But we kept trying to find my father, hoping he'd been washed ashore somewhere. I wanted to haul out the rowboat and search on the water, but no one would let me. The millpond churned wickedly under the storm surge. No boat would survive the maelstrom at its center. No boat and no person, I realized, my tears mixing with the rain soaking my cheeks.

The farmer's wife took me home and tucked me into bed, giving me hot tea to drink and whispering soothingly to me until I fell asleep. My dreams were full of black cats, severed arms, and Faye's dancing broom, punctuated by my father's final scream as the dam broke underneath him.

It took them two days to find my father's drowned body at the far end of the pond, near the witch woods from which Faye had emerged in her magic boat. Tangled up in his clothes, they found the severed paw of a black cat.

There isn't much else to tell. The farmer and his wife took me in and raised me as their own. I went on to high school and eventually married my sweetheart and settled down in Edenton. I never went back to the mill, though, close as it was to my new home. The memories there were too painful, even now.

But I still sometimes wonder what happened to Faye.

Resources

Asfar, Daniel. *Ghost Stories of America*. Edmonton, Canada: Ghost House Books, 2001.

Barefoot, Daniel W. *Haints of the Hills*. Winston-Salem, NC: John F. Blair, Publishers, 2002.

———. *Piedmont Phantoms*. Winston-Salem, NC: John F. Blair, Publishers, 2002.

———. *Seaside Spectres*. Winston-Salem, NC: John F. Blair, Publishers, 2002.

Battle, Kemp P. *Great American Folklore*. New York: Doubleday, 1986.

Botkin, B. A., ed. *A Treasury of American Folklore*. New York: Crown, 1944.

Brewer, J. Mason. *American Negro Folklore*. Chicago: Quadrangle Books, 1972.

Brown, D. *Legends*. Eugene: Randall V. Mills Archive of Northwest Folklore at the University of Oregon, 1971.

Brunvand, Jan Harold. *The Choking Doberman and Other Urban Legends*. New York: W. W. Norton, 1984.

———. *The Vanishing Hitchhiker*. New York: W. W. Norton, 1981

Coffin, Tristram P., and Hennig Cohen, eds. *Folklore in America*. New York: Doubleday & AMP, 1966.

———. *Folklore from the Working Folk of America*. New York: Doubleday, 1973.

Cohen, Daniel, and Susan Cohen. *Hauntings and Horrors*. New York: Dutton Children's Books, 2002.

Cooper, Horton. *North Carolina Mountain Folklore and Miscellany.* Murfreesboro, NC: Johnson Publishing, 1972.

Cornplanter, J. J. *Legends of the Longhouse.* Philadelphia: J. B. Lippincott, 1938.

Dorson, R. M. *America in Legend.* New York: Pantheon Books, 1973.

Downer, Deborah L. *Classic American Ghost Stories.* Little Rock, AR: August House Publishers, 1990.

Editors of Life. *The Life Treasury of American Folklore.* New York: Time, 1961.

Erdoes, Richard, and Alfonso Ortiz. *American Indian Myths and Legends.* New York: Pantheon Books, 1984.

Flanagan, J. T., and A. P. Hudson. *The American Folk Reader.* New York: A. S. Barnes, 1958.

Hardin, John. *The Devil's Tramping Ground and Other North Carolina Mystery Stories.* Chapel Hill: University of North Carolina Press, 1949.

———. *Tar Heel Ghosts.* Chapel Hill: University of North Carolina Press, 1954.

Jones, Loyal, and Billy Edd Wheeler. *Curing the Cross-Eyed Mule.* Atlanta, GA: August House Publishers, 1989.

King, Duance H., ed. *The Memoirs of Lt. Henry Timberlake.* Cherokee, NC: Museum of the Cherokee Indian Press, 2007.

Leach, M. *The Rainbow Book of American Folk Tales and Legends.* New York: World Publishing, 1958.

Leeming, David, and Jake Pagey. *Myths, Legends, and Folktales of America.* New York: Oxford University Press, 1999.

Manly, Roger. *Weird Carolinas*. New York: Sterling Publishing, 2007.

Norman, Michael, and Beth Scott. *Historic Haunted America*. New York: Tor Books, 1995.

Peck, Catherine, ed. *A Treasury of North American Folk Tales*. New York: W. W. Norton, 1998.

Polley, J., ed. *American Folklore and Legend*. New York: Reader's Digest Association, 1978.

Reevy, Tony. *Ghost Train!* Lynchburg, VA: TLC Publishing, 1998.

Renegar, Michael. *Roadside Revenants and Other North Carolina Ghosts and Legends*. Fairview, NC: Bright Mountain Books, 2005.

Roberts, Nancy. *Ghosts of the Carolinas*. Columbia: University of South Carolina Press, 1962.

———. *North Carolina Ghosts and Legends*. Columbia: University of South Carolina Press, 1959.

Rule, Leslie. *Coast to Coast Ghosts*. Kansas City, KS: Andrews McMeel Publishing, 2001.

Russel, Randy, and Janet Barnett. *Mountain Ghost Stories and Curious Tales of Western North Carolina*. Winston-Salem, NC: John F. Blair, Publisher, 1988.

Schwartz, Alvin. *Scary Stories to Tell in the Dark*. New York: Harper Collins, 1981.

Skinner, Charles M. *American Myths and Legends*. Vol. 1. Philadelphia: J. B. Lippincott, 1903.

———. *Myths and Legends of Our Own Land*. Vols. 1–2. Philadelphia: J. B. Lippincott, 1896.

Spence, Lewis. *North American Indians: Myths and Legends Series*. London: Bracken Books, 1985.

Students of Haskell Institute. *Myths, Legends, Superstitions of North American Indian Tribes.* Cherokee, NC: Cherokee Publications, 1995.

Tanenbaum, Linda Duck, and Barry McGee. *Ghost Tales from the North Carolina Piedmont.* Winston-Salem, NC: Bandit Books, 2002.

Thay, Edrick. *Ghost Stories of North Carolina.* Auburn, WA: Lone Pine Publishing International, 2005.

―――. *Ghost Stories of the Old South.* Auburn, WA: Lone Pine Publishing International, 2003.

Walser, Richard. *North Carolina Legends.* Raleigh: Office of Archives and History, North Carolina Department of Cultural History, 1980.

Whedbee, Charles Harry. *Blackbeard's Cup and Stories of the Outer Banks.* Winston-Salem, NC: John F. Blair, Publisher, 1989.

―――. *The Flaming Ship of Ocracoke and Other Tales of the Outer Banks.* Winston-Salem, NC: John F. Blair, Publisher, 1971.

―――. *Legends of the Outer Banks and Tar Heel Tidewater.* Winston-Salem, NC: John F. Blair, Publisher, 1966.

―――. *Outer Banks Mysteries and Seaside Stories.* Winston-Salem, NC: John F. Blair, Publisher, 1978.

―――. *Outer Banks Tales to Remember.* Winston-Salem, NC: John F. Blair, Publisher, 1985.

White, D. *Folk Narratives.* Eugene: Randall V. Mills Archive of Northwest Folklore at the University of Oregon, 1971.

White, Newman Ivey, ed. *The Frank C. Brown Collection of North Carolina Folklore.* Durham, NC: Duke University Press, 1958.

Zeitlin, Steven J., Amy J. Kotkin, and Holly Cutting Baker. *A Celebration of American Family Folklore.* New York: Pantheon Books, 1982.

Zeple, Terrance. *Best Ghost Tales of North Carolina.* Sarasota, FL: Pineapple Press, 2006.

———. *Ghosts of the Carolina Coasts.* Sarasota, FL: Pineapple Press, 1999.

About the Author

S. E. Schlosser has been telling stories since she was a child, when games of "let's pretend" quickly built themselves into full length tales acted out with friends. A graduate of Houghton College, the Institute of Children's Literature, and Rutgers University, she created and maintains the award-winning Web site Americanfolklore.net, where she shares a wealth of stories from all fifty states, some dating back to the origins of America. She spends much of her time answering questions from visitors to the site. Many of her favorite e-mails come from other folklorists who delight in practicing the old tradition of "who can tell the tallest tale."

About the Illustrator

Artist Paul Hoffman trained in painting and printmaking, with his first extensive illustration work on assignment in Egypt, drawing ancient wall reliefs for the University of Chicago. His work graces books of many genres—children's titles, textbooks, short story collections, natural history volumes, and numerous cookbooks. For *Spooky North Carolina,* he employed a scratchboard technique and an active imagination.